PANCHO VILLA: A *Biography*

PANCHO VILLA: A Biography

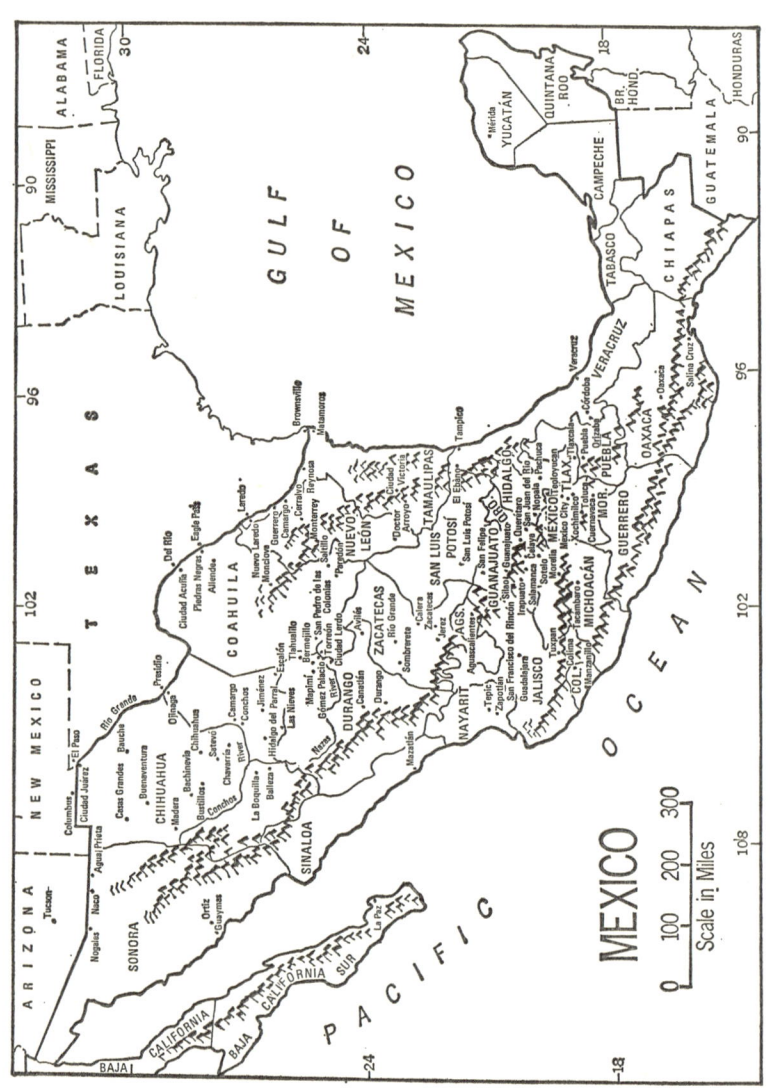

PANCHO VILLA

A Biography

by
Jean Rouverol

DOUBLEDAY & COMPANY, INC., GARDEN CITY, NEW YORK

ISBN: 0-385-00638-1 Trade
      0-385-06188-9 Prebound
Library of Congress Catalog Card Number 70-180104
Copyright © 1972 by Jean Rouverol
All Rights Reserved
Printed in the United States of America

CONTENTS

PART ONE:	THE MAKING OF AN OUTLAW	1
PART TWO:	THE MOLDING OF A SOLDIER	29
PART THREE:	BETRAYALS	63
PART FOUR:	REVOLUTION REKINDLED	95
PART FIVE:	TURMOIL	137
PART SIX:	DEFEATS	161
PART SEVEN:	THE TAMED PUMA	193
GLOSSARY		203
BIBLIOGRAPHY		207

PANCHO VILLA: A *Biography*

PART ONE

*The Making of
an Outlaw*

CHAPTER 1

HE WAS NOT born Pancho Villa. The archives of the state of Durango, on the north-central plateau of Mexico, tell the story:
"In San Juan del Río, the 7th of July, 1878, before me . . . the judge of the civil court, Agustín Arango presented himself, together with witnesses . . . and stated: That at three o'clock in the afternoon of the fifth of the preceding June, a child was born in Río Grande, to whom the name Doroteo was given. He is the legitimate son of Arango and Micaela Arámbula . . . natives of this place. . . ."
It was a matter of some pride to Doroteo, later, that he had been born legitimate. Río Grande was, after all, little more than a collection of huts on the edge of one of Durango's vast *haciendas*, and marriage was a luxury few peasants and ranch hands could afford.
Nor would one guess, from the poverty of those huts, how much of the district of San Juan del Río was rich and fertile. Jagged peaks of the Sierra Madres caught the rain clouds from the Pacific; and during the summer downpours, the Nazas and San Juan rivers filled to overflowing, washing out roads, but irrigating the valleys. Crops grew, and along the grassy

slopes of the sierra, cattle grazed. The farmland and the cattle, however, belonged to a few big landholders, not to the Indians and *mestizos* who lived and worked there.

A child growing up in that region before the turn of the century would never question such a state of affairs; it was as inevitable as life, death and poverty; as unchangeable as the landscape around him.

Indeed, the landscape itself was strange enough, the rolling hills of the sierra interrupted by twisted buttes and gorges and ravines. Here, outlined against the sky, were the Sierra de la Silla and Sierra del Gamón—Saddle Mountain and the Mountain of the Daffodil. Young Doroteo, ranging about on foot or on horseback, learned the territory like the back of his hand: the grazing country and the wooded; the foothills, and the caves and *barrancas*—the natural hiding places of wild animals and outlaws. He would, in time, have need of the knowledge; but in his childhood it was simply his *tierra*, his land.

He didn't go to school. He didn't expect to. What boy did, whose father lived in a kind of perpetual debt-slavery to the *hacienda* store? Doroteo couldn't read or write, but he picked up other knowledge. He learned about his environment by experiencing it physically. He learned how to handle a knife and a gun, and how to hunt. From the *arrieros*, the cowboys on the *hacienda*, he learned how to handle cattle, to shoe horses, to slaughter and dry meat. Also from the *arrieros*, who got about from place to place more than the farm workers did, he picked up other bits of information. He heard about Chihuahua, to the north, which had been ruled for several generations by the Terrazas family, ruthless and powerful cattle barons. There were mines in Chihuahua, too, of silver and iron, where peons toiled as they had done in the days of the Spaniards; and deserts, where the bite of the little blond scorpion could kill you in half-an-hour.

Maybe he heard about the Pacific Ocean, which a Durango

The Making of an Outlaw

peasant's son would probably never see. Or about the city of Mexico, many days' ride to the south, where the President lived, the all-powerful President who had been in office since before Doroteo's birth.

And, as he grew, Doroteo could not have helped learning one thing more. That no matter how hard a peon labored, he only went deeper into debt to the *hacienda* store. That when a father died, his debt was inherited by his son; and if a man tried to escape this bondage, he was hunted down by the hated *rurales*, the rural police, who were at the beck and call of the *hacendados*.

Unspoken, but understood, was also the fact that the *hacendado*, the owner of the *hacienda*, was the absolute ruler of the lives and honor of the people who tilled his soil.

The year 1894 found the Arango family living on the *hacienda* Gogojito, near the village of Canatlán, some thirty or forty miles from San Juan del Río. This land too, like the *hacienda* near where Doroteo had been born, belonged to the wealthy and powerful Lopez Negrete family.

Doroteo's family was fatherless, now; the older Arango had died four years earlier, and Doroteo, now sixteen, had assumed responsibility for his widowed mother, his brothers Antonio and Hipólito, and his two young sisters, Marianita and Martina. Doroteo had been sharecropping a small portion of the Lopez land, but it had been a bad season. There was no harvest—only grass, to be chopped for fodder. It was thankless work, but what else could an illiterate sixteen-year-old do, with a family of five to support, no money, and no possessions apart from a horse of sorts and an old pistol? A man labored as he had to, with no thought of trying to change his lot.

Circumstance, however, was about to change it for Doroteo.

He came in from the fields one hot day in late September,

passing in front the carriage of don Agustín Lopez Negrete, with four or five servants lounging nearby. As he came into the shadowy hut, he realized that his mother had her arm around twelve-year-old Martina; Martina's face was tracked with tears, and her mother seemed to be defending her from the landlord.

"Señor!" the widow was saying, anguished. "Get out of this house! What do you want with my daughter? Haven't you any shame?"

Doroteo realized what had happened. Blind with rage, he whirled and ran from the room, ran to his cousin's house nearby, stormed inside and took his pistol down from its rack on the wall. He ran back to his own hut and pumped three bullets into don Agustín—not killing him outright, but wounding him seriously. Don Agustín cried out for help, and the servants who had been loafing outside came running in, readying their carbines.

"Don't kill the boy!" ordered the injured man. "Just get me to the house!" The men put up their guns and carried their master out to the carriage; in a moment its wheels were raising a cloud of dust along the road to the *hacienda* of Santa Isabel de Berros, where don Agustín's wounds could be treated.

Doroteo began to come to his senses. Realizing with some surprise that he was still free, and knowing that Agustín Lopez Negrete was badly hurt, he followed his one impulse: to flee. He ran back outside to his horse, mounted, and pointed the animal's nose toward the Sierra de la Silla, which loomed not too far beyond the *hacienda* of Gogojito.

That night, he slept in the open, in the sierra.

The following day, he made his cautious way out of hiding, down from the hills, and to the hut of a friend, to ask about don Agustín.

The Making of an Outlaw

His friend shook his head. "I hear he's in bad shape. And they've sent armed men from Canatlán, to look for you."

Doroteo realized there might, of course, be reprisals against his family. "Tell my mother," he said, "to take the family to the house at Río Grande."

He knew that from now on he would be hunted by the rural police; that they would have orders to take him, dead or alive. That he would have to live a fugitive, concealed among the buttes or the *barrancas* like a coyote or mountain lion. He had fought to protect the honor of his family, and this was the result.

He said goodbye to his friend, and started back to the sierra.

That year, 1894—the year Doroteo was thrust into outlawry—there was great rejoicing in the nation's capital. From the elegant offices of the Palacio Nacional, edging the vast central plaza of Mexico City, President Díaz's government issued a proud announcement. For the first time in the country's history, read the banner headlines, Mexico had achieved a balanced budget.

CHAPTER 2

YES, THE BUDGET was balanced; and for the mine-owners and the *hacendados*, for politicians and foreign investors, it seemed a time of order and tranquillity in Mexico. President Porfirio Díaz's firm hand had indeed brought stability to the troubled country.

But at what cost to the Mexican people? How many of them, like Doroteo Arango, had been driven to outlawry—or starvation? It had been some seventy years since Mexico had won her freedom from Spain. What had gone wrong?

First of all, during their three centuries' occupation of Mexico, the Spaniards had plundered and exploited the country. They had sacked the Mexican hills of gold and silver and less precious metals, and sent them back to Spain. Ignoring their own laws against slavery, they had made slaves of the Indians, kept them working the mines and fields and building exquisite cathedrals with forced labor. They had forbidden Mexican farmers to grow any crops which might compete with those of the mother country, and had forbidden Mexican craftsmen to make anything that Spanish artisans could make. Except for a few schools and colleges operated by sympathetic *padres*, there was no education available for the Mexican peasant.

Villages, generally, were under the tyrannical control of local *caciques*, chieftains; but neither Mexicans nor creoles—those Spaniards unlucky enough to have been born in Mexico—could hold public office.

Then came 1810, and the sound of churchbells clanging one September morning in the village of Dolores, in Querétaro. The villagers, pouring into the town plaza, heard Father Hidalgo utter his famous *"Grito"*—his cry, exhorting them to throw off the yoke of the hated Spaniards and to reclaim the land which had been stolen from them three hundred years before.

For the next eleven years, the country had been swept by war, at terrible cost in lives, in ruined farmland, in hopes and ideals. Nor was peace, when it came, much better.

The country's treasury was empty. Presidents came and went; there were frequent palace coups and barracks revolts. Whenever a beleaguered administration could not meet its payroll, soldiers and politicians rose up to replace it with another. The Church owned almost half the real estate in the country, on which it paid no taxes. And one President, Santa Anna, betrayed Mexico time and again, at last inviting a United States invasion which cost his country half its total area—Texas, California, and all the land between.

The *haciendas*, however, got bigger. Churches and monasteries blazed with riches; but over the decades, the people got poorer. Freedom from Spain, it seemed, could not cure all the country's ills. One could not eat freedom.

At length, in midcentury, a group of idealists came to power—men who believed in liberty and justice. They wrote a new constitution, granting Mexicans the same privileges as those contained in the United States Bill of Rights. Public schools were created, breaking the Church's stranglehold on education. The people were to be allowed freedom of thought and religion and a free press. And, in an effort to stimulate Mexico's farming and industry, the Church's vast holdings—

which for the most part lay idle and unproductive—were put up for public sale.

Even though the Church would receive the money from such sales, however, the clergy was outraged. It could not accept the loss of its power over the state, or over the minds of the Mexican people. Once more, a combination of clergy, wealthy landowners, and much of the army rebelled against the government. Once again, the rebels invited foreign intervention; and early in the 1860s, foreign warships entered the harbor of Veracruz, and French armies swept through Mexico.

A gentle Zapotec Indian lawyer, Benito Juárez, was the country's legal President at the time; he directed the fight to repel the invaders. One of his most effective generals was another Indian from Oaxaca, a half-educated, determined young fighter named Porfirio Díaz. In time they, and others like them, succeeded in driving the French out of the country; and Maximilian, France's puppet "Emperor of Mexico," fell before a firing squad. At long last, Juárez could lead his country back to peace and to conformity with the new laws of the land.

Alas, however, the new laws said nothing about redistribution of land to the peasants, nor of seed and tools with which to farm it. Small Mexican farmers could not pay for the vast plots of Church land which were up for sale; only foreigners and the already wealthy *hacendados* could afford such prices. Even the *ejidos*—public lands the peasants had used ever since the Spanish conquest—were in many cases bought up by private interests.

So, once again, the rich got richer, and the poor got poorer. Mexico had its independence, and now at last a measure of justice too. But economically, the Mexican peasants were no better off than before.

Then, during the 1870s, President Juárez died in office,

The Making of an Outlaw

and within two years, General Porfirio Díaz "declared" against his successor.

Most of the army went over to Díaz, and in 1876 the tough, ambitious Indian came to power. It was a dictatorship that would last, with only a four-year respite, for the next thirty-four years. During those years Mexico would lose all semblance of freedom and democracy, and the peasants' and peons' hopes for economic opportunity would be ruthlessly suppressed.

It was during Díaz's regime that Doroteo had been born, grown wise in the terrain of the sierra, and committed his first "crime." Before Díaz left office, however, the young outlaw would be forged into a mighty adversary of the system which had made him what he was.

CHAPTER 3

AT FIRST, DOROTEO was lucky. In the sierra, there were caves to sleep in when it rained; deer or rabbit to kill, or wild turkey, or sometimes a stray calf. He learned to eat his meat without salt, and to dry what he could not eat immediately. The streams and springs of the sierra gave him water. He roamed where he wanted—avoiding the towns, of course—and grew as tough and wily as any of the wild animals of the mountains.

—Or almost. Perhaps, as the months went by, he became overconfident. In any event, in a moment of carelessness, he let himself be captured; and late one night, was brought down into San Juan del Río and clapped in jail.

There was no question of trial. That sort of justice existed for the rich man or the foreigner. Any peon knew what would happen in Doroteo's case: he would be taken out of doors by the *comandante* tomorrow, and shot "while attempting to escape." It was known as the *ley fuga*, "the law of the fugitive." What Doroteo did not know was that during Díaz's long presidency, the *ley fuga* would be applied more than ten thousand times.

That night, in the stifling confines of San Juan's *calabozo*,

The Making of an Outlaw

Doroteo passed what must have been the longest night of his life. At ten the next morning, one of his jailers came for him.

But it was not quite time for the execution; the guards hadn't had their breakfast yet. They sat Doroteo down outside with a barrel of corn and a stone mortar and pestle, and put him to work grinding dried corn for tortillas.

But the grinding stone had more uses than one. Doroteo watched for his chance, and then, with a force born of desperation, brought it down on the head of one of the guards, killing him with a single blow. Within moments he was heading back for the Cerro de los Remedios and its protective cover.

He didn't question the morality of the killing. An outlaw lived on the brink of extinction, where it was kill or be killed. All he thought of, as he made his way farther into the hills, was that time was on his side; the police had lost precious minutes in the confusion, and could never catch up with him now.

By the river he found a wild colt, and rode him upstream till the animal tired, then turned him loose. He walked on till he reached his birthplace, Río Grande, where—careful not to be seen—he sought out a cousin, who equipped him with horse, saddle, and a little food. Then he made his way on to the Sierra de la Silla, and took up again his life in the wilds.

Living thus, from day to day, a man keeps no track of time. Doroteo didn't think too far ahead, nor question how long he would scrape out this lonely, animal existence. But sometime during the year he passed there, he decided to give himself a new identity, in case he was caught again. He named himself "Villa," after his father's father. He would be, henceforth, Francisco Villa—Pancho for short.

The new name, however, didn't protect him from a second mishap. An acquaintance who remembered him under his old name betrayed him to the authorities; and Pancho, napping in an open field one fine October morning in 1895, woke to find himself looking into the barrels of seven carbines. He surrendered, promptly.

But he was in no hurry to see jail again. "What's all the fuss?" he asked his captors, innocently. "Let's roast a few ears of corn before we go wherever you're taking me . . ."

It didn't seem a bad idea, and the corn grew near at hand. The *comandante* shrugged: Why not? "What's there to worry about with this poor creature?" he asked his men. "All right, gentlemen. Let's roast some corn, have breakfast with him, and then take him in to San Juan del Río." What the *comandante* did not know was that there was a saddle hidden among the furrows, that a pistol lay under the blanket on which Pancho had been sleeping, and that the outlaw's horse was grazing behind the scrub a few hundred yards away.

Two of the men went to cut the corn. Two others wandered off to pick up some firewood. Pancho pulled his gun on the three who remained.

They dove for a gully, and Pancho ran to saddle and bridle his horse. By the time the seven were assembled to give chase, he was halfway to his hiding place in the mountains; he could look down over the field spread out below, and see them looking up after him, helpless.

There were other close calls before that year ended. A band of rural police—splendid in gray uniforms, red ties flying, sunlight glinting off silver buttons, gloved and hatted—rode out of Canatlán one morning to track down the outlaw. But they were not familiar with the terrain, and Pancho was. He drew them into ambush, and shot three of them. In the resulting turmoil, he had no trouble making his escape.

This time, however, he knew he must stay well away from civilization for a while. He stole a dozen head of cattle, and led them into a gorge of Hell's Canyon, where he slaughtered them and dried the meat. He would not need to venture down

The Making of an Outlaw

near a town for months, now; and some of the meat he could trade with friendly woodcutters of the area, in exchange for coffee and tortillas.

Five more months passed, and one night he crept down from Saddle Mountain to visit a friend who worked on the *hacienda* of Santa Isabel de Berros, to find out if there was any news.

"There's a lot," said his friend. "They're still looking for you." He, far better than Pancho, understood the dead-end quality of his friend's perilous existence. He mentioned a couple of outlaws he knew. "I'll get you together with them, if you want, so you won't have to go on with this dreary life you're leading. If you're interested, I'll have them here tomorrow night."

Pancho was interested. Accordingly, the following night, he was introduced to two men, fugitives like himself: Ignacio Parra—already a famous *bandido* in the area—and Refugio Alvarez.

The two bandits were uneasy when they realized how young their would-be recruit was. He stood before them: not yet eighteen—a sturdy body, without an ounce of extra flesh, but short-necked and broad-shouldered. A wide face, already burnt to leather by the sun and wind. Chestnut hair, and strange intense brown eyes with amber flecks in them; a *mestizo*, of mixed Spanish and Indian blood. He obviously considered himself a man already; but the two *bandidos* weren't so sure.

They tried to discourage him. It was their business, they said, to rob and kill. And if he joined them, he must do exactly what they ordered. Pancho agreed.

His first task, they told him, was to rustle a herd of mules from the pasture of a nearby *hacienda*. He acquitted himself to the older men's satisfaction, and before dawn the three of them, and the herd of mules, were traveling north. Pancho at last had *compañeros*—companions.

They moved at night, avoiding the roads. This part of the countryside was new to Pancho, but Ignacio and Refugio knew it well, charting their course not by roads nor by the towns they passed, but by the *haciendas*. In a few nights they had passed the *hacienda* of Canutillo, and on the last night reached the village of Ojito, "The Little Eye," where a friend of the older outlaws provided shelter for the men and pasturage for the animals.

For eight nights, Pancho slept indoors, under a roof.

When the mules were sold, Ignacio gave Pancho his share of the proceeds—three thousand pesos (worth about fifteen hundred dollars). Pancho was staggered. In all his life he had never had more than a hundred at one time. He set off straightway for town, and bought himself a whole new wardrobe.

But for all the excitement of new clothes and the pleasure of having cash in his pockets, Pancho was uneasy; he longed to be back in familiar country. Ignacio at last set a night for their departure, but pointed out that Pancho still didn't have the one thing he needed most for the journey—a good horse.

Pancho pondered the advice. He started into town, to see what he could find, and stopped short when he saw tethered just in front of the *cantina*'s door, as if in answer to his dream, a magnificent black horse, with a new saddle and bridle.

Without a second thought, he mounted the animal and started off at his leisure, when he heard a shout behind him: "Hey, you! Where do you think you're going!" Pancho didn't wait to answer; he simply dug his heels into the animal's sides and they sped back to the corral in the countryside where the mules had been pastured.

So now, at last, he had a fine new mount, and it hadn't cost him a centavo. What was more, his show of enterprise had earned his companions' respect. He was ready to go home.

At the little hut in Río Grande, his mother received him with the same tenderness she had always shown him. But when he handed her the sheaves of pesos—all he had left from his share of the sale of the mules—she was visibly upset, and asked him where in the world he had gotten so much money.
She didn't really need to ask; she knew the answer. Those two men he traveled with, she said, were leading him straight to damnation.
Pancho was defensive. He was born to suffer, he said; it was his destiny. "I don't expect anyone to forgive me. My enemies would like to see me dead." He reminded her how it had all begun—he'd committed his first crime only to defend his family. "The truth is," he said, "I would rather be the number one bandit of the world, than allow my family's honor to be dragged in the mud." He begged her to give him her blessing, and to commend him to God's care. God would know well enough, he said, what to do with him.

CHAPTER 4

ON PANCHO'S NEXT visit home, he brought a still larger sum: what was left of fifty thousand pesos, after a good deal of general celebration. He gave a great wad of the bills to his family, and then, in a burst of sympathy for a half-blind tailor he knew, bought and equipped a tailoring shop, with a man to do the sewing, so the tailor's large and hungry family needn't starve. Within eight or ten months he had given away, just as impulsively, all the rest of the money.

He wasn't worried. There was more where that came from.

There were disadvantages to such a life, however. One morning, again at the entrance to Hell's Canyon, the three outlaws were found asleep by a handful of hunters, and Pancho and Refugio were both nicked by bullets before they could escape. Another time, the three were forced to shoot their way clear of a sixty-man posse.

There were triumphs, and betrayals. One always sought out the betrayer, and took revenge; or repaid a kindness with a fistful of pesos, or by pausing a month or two to help a good man bring in his harvest. The bandits roamed wide through the area, and Pancho increased his knowledge of the sierra's secrets—the passes, the watering places; box canyons useful

The Making of an Outlaw

for ambush, and the open plateaus, the hills, and the *arroyos*. One stole what one could, killed when one had to. And sometimes—perhaps inevitably—one quarreled with a friend.

The quarrel with Refugio happened when one of Pancho's mules stumbled and rolled over a cliff, carrying a load of meat the men had stolen and dried. Refugio, angered, burst out in a string of curses, blaspheming not only Pancho but Pancho's innocent—and absent—mother. Pancho went into one of his sudden rages and shot Refugio's horse out from under him, leaving the older outlaw at the bottom of the cliff, horseless, gunless, and begging for mercy.

They never saw each other again. A few months later, they heard that during a cattle-rustling incident at a nearby ranch, Refugio had been betrayed by the foreman and killed in a shoot-out. Pancho and Ignacio sought out the foreman and killed him.

Not long after, Pancho quarreled with Ignacio, over the shooting of a poor old man who was carrying a load of bread to the *hacienda* Santa Isabel. The old man had refused to sell them any of the bread, and had been shot for his obstinacy. Pancho was angry at the killing, which seemed to him unnecessary, and threatened to ride on alone. Ignacio merely shrugged. "Go whenever you like," he said. "But you'll never make it without me."

Pancho said nothing. He simply reined his horse about and rode away. He had survived alone in the sierra before, and he could do it again.

For a while, he lived in the sierra by himself. Then he took on a *compadre* who cheated him; and another, Luis Orozco, who proved more loyal. But Pancho by now was well known to the authorities throughout Durango, and the *rurales* were after him ceaselessly. At length he decided he'd had his fill.

Accordingly, he and his friend made their way north, and crossed over the state border into Chihuahua, where they stopped at the ancient Spanish mining town of Hidalgo del Parral. Orozco got homesick after a month or two, and went back to his *tierra;* but Pancho—finding himself unrecognized for a change—went to work in the mines.

He had been at work only a few weeks when a rock crushed his foot. He assumed the wound would heal itself, but gangrene set in. Treatments from a doctor in Parral cost him his horse, his saddle and bridle, his rifle, even his blanket; and when all his money was gone, the doctor refused him any further treatment. Pancho tried to cure the foot himself. By now, he was too poor even to afford a place to sleep, and was forced to take shelter in holes in the hillside where limestone had been quarried. Mornings, he woke to the sound of the six o'clock work whistles, and limped—still in pain—down to the public market, hoping someone would offer him something to eat.

At this low point in his life, a stranger came to his aid.

His name was Santos Vega; he was a master brickmason, engaged on several building jobs in Parral. He chanced to notice Pancho one morning in the marketplace, and asked him if he wanted to work. Pancho said yes. Vega suspected that the ragged, ravaged-looking young man was hungry, and gave him a peso for breakfast. Then, as they started toward the railroad station, he noticed that Pancho was limping, and when he saw the ugly wound, and realized Pancho had no family, he gave him a job breaking up bricks for riprap, for a peso a day.

The easy money of Pancho's bandit days was forgotten. A peso a day—about fifty cents—meant the difference between eating and starving. Pancho went to work with a will.

As the days went by, he got to know some poor old women living near the railroad. He gave them his daily peso, and they took care of him. When Santos Vega's doctor wanted to amputate Pancho's gangrenous leg, they refused to allow it, and cured it themselves with herbs and hot compresses.

The Making of an Outlaw

Pancho himself, ashamed of his appearance, dragged himself every week to a hill above Parral, to do his washing in a stream.

When he was able to work on his feet, he joined the other peons stacking adobe brick. But he was eager for more responsibility, and urged Vega to let him use the trowel. Soon he was doing a mason's work, for a mason's pay; and in a short time more, Vega made him supervisor over several small jobs—dividing the proceeds with him, share and share alike. It looked as though Pancho had, at last, found a new and honest life for himself.

But, inevitably, came the day when the police *comandante* dropped by the job where Pancho and Vega were working, and spoke to Vega privately. When he had gone, Vega said the *comandante* had asked about Pancho—who he was, and whether he came from Durango; there was a request out, he said, for the extradition of a man answering Pancho's description. It was only out of respect for Vega that the *comandante* had not arrested Pancho on the spot.

That afternoon, Pancho collected the horse, saddle, and pistol which his earnings had bought him, and came to say goodbye to his employer. Then he set out, once again, for the sierra.

Near the Durango border, he stopped at an *hacienda* where an old friend of his was working—Eleuterio Soto, a man he had always liked and whose courage he respected. Soto insisted on traveling with him, and together they rode south, toward the village of Río Grande. Pancho hoped to see his mother; he had been without news of her for a long time.

But the news, when he got it, was not good. He and Soto had paused near the *hacienda* of Santa Isabel de Berros, and encountered one of Pancho's brothers. The boy had come to fetch his sister Martina, who worked as a maid there now, for their mother was very sick.

Pancho told him to get Martina, and take her home. But he dared not follow quite yet; if anyone had seen him riding in, they would be on the lookout for him at the Arango house. "I'll come tomorrow night," he said.

The following night, still worried that the *rurales* might be watching his family's place, Pancho stopped at a hut nearby—and was told that his mother had died.

From where he stood, he could make out his own house. There were lights in the window. They were, he knew, candles for the dead; his brother and sister would be keeping vigil by his mother's body. He had not been able to be at her side, he thought bitterly, even when she lay dying.

For a long time, he looked at the pinpoints of light in the darkness. Then, at last, he went outside and untethered his horse. He mounted, and reined the animal north, toward Chihuahua.

There was no particular hurry now. He rode away from the dark huddle of huts at a walk, crying as he rode.

CHAPTER 5

KNOWING THEY NEEDED fresh horses, the outlaws stole two fine ones from a *rancho* along the way. But when they arrived at the *hacienda* where Eleuterio had lived, they found that in Eleuterio's absence, the *hacendado* had accused him of all the unsolved crimes in the neighborhood.

Eleuterio was furious. A little horse-thievery was one thing; the heinous crimes he was accused of were quite another. Sure he could prove his innocence, he let himself be arrested and jailed.

But justice belonged to the rich, not the poor. Under heavy pressure from the *hacendado*, the judge convicted Eleuterio and sentenced him to be shot. Because of the cowboy's good reputation among the local *rancheros*, however, the sentence was reduced to service in the army.

It was a common punishment. Men of influence frequently used this means of getting rid of anyone who proved a nuisance: a troublesome employee, for instance; or a husband or father who stood in the way of some attractive young peasant girl . . . So, in short order, Eleuterio found himself in uniform, in an army barracks in Mexico City.

There was, at least, a cure for that problem. One could pay

a substitute to serve one's time. Pancho sent his friend enough money to buy his way out of the army and come home. And within two days of his return, Eleuterio sought out his persecutor the *hacendado* and filled him with bullets. This time there was no doubt about his guilt.

Back in the hills again, the two men tried to think of some way to make an honest living. But Pancho had learned, by now, that on a daily wage, a man could starve; it was better to be one's own boss. He and Soto contracted for the slaughter and sale of three hundred cattle, outside Parral; and with their profits, continued north toward the town of Chihuahua, where with luck they might pass unrecognized. Pancho had an idea that he might open a meat market. Soto dreamed he might be able to bring his family north . . .

He did. For a year, the two men labored. Pancho had planned to use the city's slaughterhouse, and sell his own meat in his own market. But even here, he was frustrated.

The slaughterhouse was controlled by two petty grafters, who always managed to find some reason for rejecting Pancho's animals and forcing him to buy their own, at exorbitant prices. Pancho was unable to make a profit; and by year's end, he realized that his problem was not unique; *politicos* seemed to have a monopoly on all the slaughtering in Chihuahua. Angry and discouraged, he abandoned the little market to a friend.

He tried working in the mines again, in the small mining town of Santa Eulalia. But the work was backbreaking, the pay miserable. After a year and a half he was poorer than when he had begun.

And somehow, while he had been toiling anonymously in the mines, the authorities in Durango had got wind of his whereabouts, and he had to flee again. There seemed to be no place for him but the sierra; and now, thanks to his efforts to support himself honestly, he had no means of survival there

The Making of an Outlaw

at all. He had had to sell his horse, his rifle, and his pistol. There was nothing left.

The problem was not beyond remedy. He returned to Chihuahua and stole a horse from under the very noses of the larcenous slaughterhouse butchers; and, together with Eleuterio and another outlaw named José Sanchez, returned to life as an outlaw. They lived, for the most part, by rustling cattle from the Terrazas *ranchos*—the hated Terrazas family, who had been overlords of Chihuahua for so many years.

But such a life meant there could be little peace for Villa. He and his companions roamed the foothills, hiding, being followed, suspecting everything and everyone. Knowing that at any moment there could be an ambush, a surprise assault . . .

At least, though, he had a few pesos in his pocket again. And, since his wanderings took him to Chihuahua so often, he thought about buying some sort of little house there where he could stay, discreetly, whenever he had cattle or meat to dispose of. After a good deal of looking, he found one on Tenth Street, on the northern edge of the city: an old place but comfortable, with three rooms of whitewashed adobe brick, and plenty of space outdoors to build a corral for his animals. It seemed exactly what he wanted.

He set to work immediately, adding a stable which he built himself, and fitting it with manger and watering trough. He did his own roofing, of thatch; and he put up the planks for a corral fence. To a man who for more than a decade had had no roof for his head, the house seemed finer than a palace; he would be fond of it as long as he lived.

Among other reasons, because it was there he met the man who was to change his life.

His name was Abraham González. Dark-haired, dark-mustached, he was already graying, though he was only a few years older than Pancho. His black eyes were alert, and his face pleasant and open—a face that had never known hardship or bitterness. González was, in fact, something altogether new to Pancho: a member of the upper classes who did not exploit the poor.

A few years before, he had imported a herd of Herefords, to improve the stock of the local *rancheros*. Since then he'd earned wide respect as a bank administrator and treasury official. He seemed the last man in the world to be a revolutionary—and yet, word was being passed around Chihuahua that that was exactly what he had become.

He had started something called the "Anti-Reelection Club" in the city; and lately, had been quietly lining up a number of *vaqueros* from the local *ranchos*, to be trained as guerrilla fighters or as cavalrymen—just in case. History does not tell how he and Pancho met, that fateful year of 1910; but Pancho's reminiscences, dictated a few years later, tell of a long conversation they held, late one quiet autumn night, in the three-room adobe on Tenth Street—a conversation that would put an end to Pancho's life as an outlaw, and provide a goal for the hitherto blind rush of his anger and resentments.

It was there in his own house, Pancho wrote, that "I came to realize how the battles I had fought for years, against those who enslaved the poor and dishonored our daughters, could serve for something good. Something which could be of help to other people who had been exploited and humiliated as I had been." He learned from González, that night, that there were other kinds of fighting than merely exchanging bullets on the streets or in the hills. And he realized, as González spoke, that the rages and hatreds that had been building up in him through so many years could change—with the belief that the evils around him could be changed.

"This belief," he said, "was like a force, a determination to find remedies, even at the cost of blood or life itself!"

The Making of an Outlaw

It was that night, in the little adobe, that he came to understand, he said, what no one had ever explained before "since nobody ever explained anything to us the poor. That what we call our fatherland—which for me had until then been only a bitter affection for the fields, the canyons, and the mountains that hid me—could be changed into a motive for our greatest efforts, and the beloved object of our deepest emotions."

And it was there, that night, that Pancho heard for the first time the name of Francisco Madero, the leader of the anti-Díaz movement. "I learned to love and revere him," he wrote of Madero, "for his unbreakable faith. For bringing us his brilliant 'Plan of San Luis,' and for showing us his desire to fight, in spite of his own wealth, for us the poor and the oppressed."

The gunfighter had at last met the intellectual. It would take both kinds of men to rid Mexico of Porfirio Díaz.

PART TWO

The Molding of a Soldier

CHAPTER 6

PORFIRIO DÍAZ HAD COME to power in Mexico in 1876. At the end of his first term in office, he had made a bow in the direction of legality by allowing another man to hold office for four years; then, in 1884, he returned to the presidency for an uninterrupted twenty-six-year reign.

To be sure, he had fought against the French under Benito Juárez, but he was no idealist. He was a soldier, and he governed like a soldier—or, more precisely, like a commanding officer who must have absolute obedience from the ranks.

Part Spanish, part Mixtecan Indian, he was only semi-literate; he was in fact not unlike the native *caciques*—bosses, or strong men—who ruled small villages with an iron hand. His philosophy of government was simple: a dog with a bone in its mouth, he said, neither kills nor steals; hence, he made sure that all his potential rivals were given important posts in the government, or a chance to get rich. If anyone opposed him seriously, the remedy was simple: "Catch in the act, kill on the spot." He wanted order and prosperity for the leaders of Mexico, and to attain them, he was willing to sacrifice justice and civil rights.

During his four years out of office, he had returned to

his native Oaxaca, and there, at the age of fifty-one, had married the sixteen-year-old daughter of one of his political followers. Carmencita Rubio de Díaz, though young, soon rid Porfirio of his Indian ways; she taught him table manners, and how to dress, and improved his grammar. And, being a devout churchgoer, she arranged a meeting between her new husband and the Archbishop of Mexico. As a result, Díaz agreed that the anti-clerical laws of the Reform would not be enforced. In very little time, the Church began acquiring land again.

By the time Díaz returned to Mexico City and the presidency, he was a new man, with the drooping white mustache and elegant bearing of a Spanish grandee. He appointed as his Secretary of Treasury don José Ives Limantour, an authentically elegant gentleman who, with Díaz, hoped to turn quiet, agricultural Mexico into a modern capitalist country. They and their fellow officials, known as *científicos*, felt that the Mexican government should be run on scientific lines. They courted British, French, and American investors; American railroad builders were offered every concession; and before long, a quarter of all the land in Mexico was in foreign hands—as well as half the oil fields and two-thirds of the mines.

Even justice belonged to the Europeans and the Americans, who could be assured of winning every legal dispute in the courts. In short, it was with good reason that Mexico became known as "the mother of foreigners, the stepmother of Mexicans."

Díaz was reelected regularly. The technique was simple. He appointed his most loyal supporters as governors of the various states. The state governments, in turn, conducted the elections and counted the ballots (often, for the benefit of the illiterate, beans to be dropped into one of two urns). Díaz couldn't lose.

And woe to any newspaperman who objected. More than

The Molding of a Soldier

half-a-dozen anti-Díaz journalists were assassinated, on order of state governors. Others, luckier, were sent to Belém penitentiary, an ancient, converted convent building in Mexico City, rife with itch, typhus, and tuberculosis; or to the damp and dripping underground cells of the island fortress San Juan Ulúa, in the harbor at Veracruz. Printers who had merely set type for the dissident writers were sent to join them. One courageous editor was sentenced to jail thirty-four times; another, who had fled to Texas for safety, survived two assassination attempts there and was killed in a third. A press in Arizona which printed stories of Mexican government atrocities was wrecked, and political refugees were arrested as far away as Los Angeles by private detectives paid by Díaz.

So, though all seemed to be at peace in Mexico under don Porfirio, in reality, as one observer said, "The peace that reigns is the peace of death."

All these problems, however, were matters for the politicians. Pancho Villa, *campesino* and outlaw, who never in his life had read a newspaper or known a politician, had realized little of it until his fateful meeting with Abraham González.

What he was all too familiar with was poverty. Most of the people he knew worked for a peso a day—some, for only a few centavos, though the price of corn for tortillas had more than quadrupled in the last hundred years. He might have known *rancheros* who had lost their few meters of cornfield because they were unable to borrow money for seed or tools; and he may, in his wanderings, have heard stories about what the government had done to the Yaqui Indians in Sonora. Or perhaps he didn't, because the whole history was so shameless that every effort was made to suppress it.

In the early 1890s, the governor of Sonora and a few of his powerful friends, including the general of the army in Mexico's northwest, determined to get possession of the fertile lands which the Yaqui had farmed since time immemorial. The Yaqui, naturally, had resisted. Díaz's government issued a decree expropriating the land and sent in troops to enforce the new law. Since then, Yaqui men, women and children had been shot, imprisoned, publically mutilated, or hanged—or, in some cases, carried by gunboat down the river and dropped into the sea.

In time, however, Sonora's governor and the army chieftain worked out a more profitable way of dealing with their stubborn adversaries. They sold them, at sixty-five dollars a head, as slaves to the great plantations in Yucatán and Quintana Roo, to produce chicle and hennequin under the broiling tropical sun. The Yaqui, bred in temperate climate, seldom survived a year of this life; but two successive governors of Sonora became multimillionaires.

All over Mexico, small *ranchitos*—indeed, whole villages—were swallowed up by land-hungry *hacendados* without even a show of legality and many of the farmers and peasants who resisted were summarily shot. In the state of Hidalgo, not far from the Mexican capital, a number of Indian farmers were buried up to their necks in their own land, and then galloped over by the horses of the rural police.

Most of Mexico's agricultural workers were too weakened, too hungry and oppressed, to rebel. But in Porfirio Díaz's desire to industrialize Mexico, a new class of Mexican was emerging: the men who worked on the railroads, or in the mines, or in the newly built factories. It was these workers who formed labor unions, and had the courage to strike against their employers. For their pains, they were shot down by the hundreds—but many survived, and remembered.

And as time went on, some of the Mexican farmers and businessmen came to resent the special concessions given foreign investors. They began to hope for a change, as did a

The Molding of a Soldier

number of young lawyers and intellectuals in and around Mexico City.

But it was a small man, hardly five feet two, with a nervous, high-pitched voice, and a gentle face with a trim brown beard, a vegetarian and a spiritualist, the eldest son of an immensely wealthy family of northern Mexico—who would be most directly responsible for Díaz's fall, when it came. His name was Francisco Madero.

He was an unworldly man, but infinitely kind. Having no children of his own, he and his wife had adopted six children and had fed, clothed, and educated many more, on his *hacienda* in Coahuila. He feared violence, and mistrusted radicals. But most of Díaz's opponents had rallied around his book *The Presidential Succession*. His later statement, the "Plan of San Luis Potosí," would let the genii of revolution out of the bottle.

Nineteen hundred and ten, the year of Pancho Villa's fateful conversation with Abraham González, was an election year. Two years before, Díaz had announced in a magazine interview his intention not to run again. Moreover, he said, he would welcome political opposition. The article had given hope to tens of thousands of his countrymen. But sure enough, when election time arrived, don Porfirio was once more a candidate. And once more, he had chosen as his running mate the most hated man in the country, Ramon Corral—a former governor of Sonora who had made a fortune selling the Yaqui into slavery, and who now was reputed to be the protector of all the vice and prostitution in Mexico City. The canny Díaz thus protected himself against assassination: no one in his right mind would want Corral to succeed to the presidency!

Francisco Madero had been nominated to oppose Díaz. At first, don Porfirio could not take the eccentric little man seriously; but as Madero went about the country exhorting his fellow citizens to vote down the Díaz dictatorship, the President became irritated. In June he had Madero thrown in jail in San Luis Potosí, and intensified his persecution of newspapermen and others who spoke against reelection. By July 8th, when voting took place, there were more than sixty thousand political prisoners in Mexican jails.

Emotions were running high, now, and everywhere there were signs of discontent. Even in Mexico City—the very center of the *científicos*—a huge group of *Maderistas* demonstrated along the elegant Paseo de la Reforma, hurling rocks through the windows of the imposing houses fronting the boulevard. They were ridden down by the police.

Undaunted, the Díaz administration pursued its plans for a glittering hundredth anniversary of Father Hidalgo's call for independence. Trainloads of champagne arrived in the capital. Every public building was strung with thousands of light bulbs, to turn the city into a fairyland of lights at night; and, on September 16th, there was a lavish reception for local and foreign dignitaries, at which doña Carmencita Rubio de Díaz presided in a gown from Paris and a necklace of pearls and diamonds. All told, the celebration cost twenty million pesos —ten million dollars. This, at a time when in the country as a whole, three-quarters of the populace were in worse economic condition than their forefathers had been in Father Hidalgo's time.

Early in October it was announced—to no one's surprise —that the eighty-year-old Díaz and his running mate Corral had won the election. At almost the same time, Madero's family managed by bail or bribe to get Madero out of jail, and smuggled him north disguised as a brakeman. On October 7th he crossed the border into Texas and published the plan he had evolved during his weeks in jail: the "Plan of San Luis Potosí." In it, he denounced the election as illegal; stated again the principle that there should be no reelection; called

The Molding of a Soldier

for a return of public (*ejidal*) lands to the villagers, and announced himself provisional President of Mexico.

And he called for a general uprising against the Díaz government, to take place November 20th—five weeks away.

Meanwhile, in Chihuahua, Pancho Villa had already had a foretaste of revolution, though at first it was hardly distinguishable from his previous gunfights as an outlaw.

He had recruited and equipped his first fifteen young revolutionaries—including his fellow outlaws Eleuterio Soto and José Sanchez. Tomás Urbina was one of them too—rowdy, bloodthirsty, but full of laughter and a good friend. With his little band in tow, Villa had sought out and "executed" a judge who was reputedly an enemy of their cause.

On his return to town he had, with his men, acted as a bodyguard to González—a wise precaution, as tensions were mounting throughout northern Mexico. Then, one night in mid-November, don Abraham had come to the house on Tenth Street where Pancho was quartering his men, had placed them under the leadership of a man named Cástulo Herrera, and ordered them up to the Sierra Azul, above the little railroad town of San Andrés, while he himself went northeast to Ojinaga, near the Texas frontier.

Before leaving, González had given each of the men a warm *abrazo*. Later, when the city was silent and asleep, the little detachment slipped quietly outside to the dark corral, saddled up, and set out.

It was, for Pancho, the most awesome moment of his life. He had not wept since the death of his mother, but he fought down tears that night, as his little band rode through the dark streets of Chihuahua City. It was not sorrow he felt, but something larger. Horses' hooves struck against cobbles; there was a muted clank of stirrups and mountings. As they drew away from the city's outskirts he wanted to shout out into the quiet dark, "*Viva* the cause of the poor! *Viva* Abraham González. *Viva* Francisco Madero!"

But a time for shouting would come later. Now was a time to ride unheard and unseen, in silence, until they reached the shelter of the hills.

CHAPTER 7

PANCHO'S EXPLOITS AS an outlaw had already made him something of a folk hero to the villagers in the hills; and when word got round that Chihuahua's *bandido número uno* wanted fighters for a revolution, men came flocking, bringing their own horses, arms and ammunition. In five days, Pancho and Herrera had winnowed the volunteers down to three hundred seventy-five men; and Herrera gave the order to move, that same night, down onto San Andrés.

At dawn they had the town surrounded. But there was no resistance; the few *rurales* stationed there had already fled. The guerrilla leaders' first act, then, was to enter the town peacefully and appoint authorities, to make sure there would be no disorder and no looting.

But the new recruits, jubilant at finding themselves within the town and already victorious, began firing wildly into the air, to celebrate. Pancho waited for Herrera to stop them; and when Herrera did nothing, Pancho shouted to them to save their fire for the enemy. "Do you think this morning is a sample of what we've got ahead of us?" he yelled. "Listen, we haven't begun to fight!"

Herrera's primary worry was the ten o'clock train, which

might be bringing unwelcome visitors from Chihuahua. At his order, Pancho chose an escort—his original fifteen recruits—and went down to the station. Already he could hear the locomotive's whistle coming nearer. He had scarcely deployed his handful of men when the train came into view—carrying a detachment of federal troops.

As it pulled into the station, Pancho's men began to shoot. There were answering shots from the train. The commanding officer of the *Federales* was killed in the first exchange of fire. Townspeople, hearing the commotion, came running to help the guerrillas; and, seeing this, the federal captains ordered the engineers to start up again. The train began to move, out of the station and past the town, carrying its dead and wounded and gathering speed as it went. It did not return.

Two days later the guerrillas repeated their easy victory at the little town of Santa Isabel. There, their ranks increased to five hundred. And command, almost imperceptibly, began to shift from Herrera to the outlaw chieftain who understood so much more about the countryside and its men. Pancho Villa was becoming the commanding officer in all but name.

But in organized warfare, he was still too raw, too inexperienced. In his exhilaration over two easy victories and an ever-expanding body of volunteers, he made a rash decision. He decided to attack Chihuahua City.

A day's march brought him within a few miles of the city. He left the main body of his forces at a nearby *hacienda*, sent some of his men to reconnoiter the surrounding highlands, and took twenty-three of his guerrillas down to Tecolote Flat, en route to the city.

There, however, they heard gunfire. As they drew closer, Villa realized that they faced several hundred federal soldiers. But it was too late to withdraw; and with a recklessness he would regret for years, he led his men in an attack—and was set upon by the federals' whole Twentieth Battalion. Realizing he was surrounded, he signaled a retreat.

The Molding of a Soldier 41

A portion of the little group managed to fight its way to safety, and straggled back to the *hacienda* to rejoin the main body of their troops. There, Pancho reckoned up the losses that his inexperience and his impulsiveness had cost him. He himself was wounded in one leg; three others were injured, and nine of the twenty-three were killed.

One of the dead was Pancho's outlaw friend José Sanchez. Another was his still closer friend, the courageous Eleuterio Soto. Soto had once promised Pancho he would stay with him to the death; he had kept the promise.

In the rest of the country, the infant revolution did not look too promising. The leader of the *Maderista* forces in Puebla, a prematurely bald young merchant named Aquiles Serdán, had been amassing weapons and ammunition for an uprising on November 20th. But two days before, the police had got wind of the plan and raided the house, killing Serdán and his brother and appropriating the weapons. Elsewhere, there were small, sporadic outbreaks: in Jalisco, to the west; in Sonora to the northwest; in Zacatecas; in Mexico City—but they were all put down with ease by the federal troops.

Madero himself was poised on the other side of the Texas border, in San Antonio; one of his uncles had promised to meet him the night of November 19th, in Coahuila, with five hundred men. Madero and a handful of friends equipped themselves with horses, arms, and ammunition, and on the appointed night, set out. But they got lost. They wandered about in the night, trying to find the Rio Grande, found it at last, and waded across—to be met by no more than two dozen men, mostly unarmed and with federal troops hot on their trail. Madero, discouraged, retreated back across the border, and in the days following, moved on to New Orleans, which had been a place of refuge for Mexican exiles since the time of Benito Juárez.

But in Chihuahua, matters were beginning to look more hopeful.

There, the power of the Terrazas family had been a daily misery for decades. There was hardly a peasant family in the state who had not suffered some injustice at their hands. For the *Chihuahuenses,* revolution meant ridding themselves, once and for all, of their hated governor Alberto Terrazas and his whole clan. President Díaz was only a name, and a distant one at that; but the Terrazas family were close at hand. They were the immediate enemy.

So there were bitter uprisings simultaneously in half a dozen areas of the state, under as many leaders. At first, it seemed, the most successful of these was not Villa, but an ambitious shopkeeper in the southern part of the state, named Pascual Orozco. Orozco was a former muleteer and wagon master: a tall, thin, humorless, almost threateningly good-looking man who had joined the revolution, not because of Madero, at whom he scoffed, but because of his abiding hatred for the Terrazas family and others like them. Early in December he had captured the city of Guerrero, about a hundred miles east of Chihuahua; and, hearing of Villa's first easy victories up north, sent him a telegram: "I've just taken this place. Come down and let me help you out with some ammunition."

Villa had just returned to San Andrés after a journey incognito into Chihuahua for supplies. He'd bought sugar and coffee—luxuries, perhaps, but urgent if he wanted to keep his men happy. The people up in San Andrés provided him with the rest of his provisions, and with feed for his horses, but the offer of ammunition tempted him and he decided to accept Orozco's invitation.

Three days' march took him to Ciudad Guerrero. The people of the area knew of him and gave him a noisy welcome. They offered to move out of their own dwellings to make room for his officers and men; but Villa and Herrera

The Molding of a Soldier 43

thought it better to make camp on the outskirts of town. This, Villa reasoned, would help assure the townspeople that the revolution was well organized and in the hands of men who were truly concerned with the comfort and welfare of their fellow Mexicans. A far cry, indeed, from the number one bandit of Durango and Chihuahua!

He and the other officers held a conference on their next move. They knew that a column of federal troops had spent the preceding night at San Nicolás and was now moving north; so it was agreed that the Revolutionary troops, with each leader in charge of his own men, would march on the federal forces. At dawn the next morning they set out.

But they were outmatched, and after heavy casualties were forced to retreat.

Still more disastrous was the loss, soon after their return, of friendly San Andrés. Federal troops infiltrated the town by way of an *arroyo*, surprising Villa and costing his men their horses, their saddles, their supplies, and even their blankets, which they left behind them as they fled.

There was snow in the sierra now, and a man without his *serape* suffered bitterly from the cold. But these men were for the most part miners and peasants; they were used to hardship and discomfort. In spite of the loss of the town and of all their possessions, every man among them followed Villa farther up into the sierra without a word of protest.

As an old cattle rustler, Villa saw to it that no matter what else his army lacked, they were never without meat. For almost a week his men survived there in the mountains, huddled together against the cold, drinking from icy streams, cooking their freshly butchered beef over charcoal, and eating it without salt. At last, at week's end, one of Villa's officers arrived from a *rancho* below with four hundred horses. When the volunteers took to the road again, they were ragged, bareback, bridling their horses with bits of rope—but at least they had horses; and before long, *haciendas* along the way provided saddles.

Villa's next attempt was against the city of Camargo. He had taken the town and all but one of the *Federales*' barracks, when word came that federal reinforcements were en route from Chihuahua. So, for the sake of his men, he abandoned the ground he had gained.

His men were still without blankets and lacked much in the way of clothing. On his withdrawal from Camargo, he invaded a company village, where a dam was being built. Villa helped himself and his men to clothes and supplies from the company store; put up his men in company hotels; and he himself rested for three days as a houseguest of the manager, who—no doubt terrified—refused even an I.O.U. from the guerrilla leader. The company was delighted, said the manager eagerly, to be of help in so noble a cause!

Well and good. But by now it was mid-February, and Villa had yet to win his first major battle.

CHAPTER 8

ON THE FOURTEENTH of that same February, 1911, Francisco Madero crossed the Rio Grande a few miles below El Paso into Chihuahua. He was met by a small group of revolutionaries which, together with his own few, gave him a total of a hundred and thirty-seven men; and with this tiny army, he set out to conquer Mexico.

He moved south, skirting sand dunes in the Chihuahua desert, wading rivers, edging bare brown hills, and living on canned beans, sardines, and soda crackers. He reached Buenaventura, where the townspeople greeted him with wild enthusiasm and volunteers swelled his ranks to five hundred. He also learned that federal troops stationed at Casas Grandes, to his northwest, had been reduced, to strengthen garrisons along the border.

Accordingly, he set out with his men to the northwest; and at Casas Grandes, near the site of an ancient, pre-Spanish abandoned village, he and his men attacked. It was now three weeks since he had reentered Mexico.

The *casas grandes*—centuries-old ruins like those of the Zuñi and Pueblo Indians—looked silently toward the battle. Things went badly for Madero. Though he showed great physical courage, he knew nothing whatever about military tactics; he was wounded in one arm and almost captured, was rescued, and finally, was forced to sound a retreat, leaving a fifth of his troops behind him, dead or wounded.

It had been his first smell of gunpowder, and a discouraging one. He and his surviving men regrouped and moved south to the *hacienda* of Bustillos, near the railroad. There, he did what he should have done in the first place—he sent for Pascual Orozco and Pancho Villa.

Orozco, a few weeks previously, had left Ciudad Guerrero and, aboard two railroad trains he had captured, had moved his troops northward for an attempt against the border town of Ciudad Juárez. The attempt, unfortunately, had failed.

Villa had put in the intervening time in minor skirmishes. As he had done at Camargo, he would take his position before a garrisoned town and send in a challenge to the commanding officer: "I want to spare villages wherever I can. Let your civilians remain, and come out like soldiers to meet Pancho Villa and his Revolutionaries!"

The answer was usually a refusal. Pancho's counteranswer was sometimes an attack, sometimes a withdrawal. Often, his target was not a village but an *hacienda*, complete with its stables, smithy, granary, mill, and company store. Here he and his men could replenish their supplies of horses, food and fodder—either with the consent of the owner or without. He kept his forces constantly on the move, making sudden strikes and just as sudden withdrawals, living off the land and never letting the enemy know where he would turn up next. It was a technique he had often used as an outlaw—but he employed it now on a much grander scale, and with far more admirable motives.

Nearing Hidalgo del Parral, he had decided to find out what kind of military installations the *Federales* had set up there. He had ridden into town on an old plug of a horse,

The Molding of a Soldier

and without his rifle and cartridge belt, hoping to look like any ordinary *campesino*. He knew, however, that on the morrow a boy would follow him into town, with a burro carrying sacks of charcoal—and with rifles hidden in the charcoal. It was well to be prepared.

There was a kind of bitter nostalgia attached to this visit. Parral was the town where he had grown from youth to man, and where the "justice of the rich" had so often deprived him of the right to make an honest living. Now he prowled about the familiar streets; discovered what he wanted to know about the enemy's installations; and at one point, in flight from a group of suspicious *Federales*, had taken refuge in the house of Santos Vega, the master mason who had fed him and given him work when he was younger.

On rejoining his men, he had made for San Andrés, now vacated again by the *Federales*; and there, early in the second week of March, had received Madero's message to come to Bustillos. To come "without his troops," the message said, but at the same time to take every precaution for his own security.

Within two hours, he was at Bustillos, to meet the man he had idolized from afar; and to learn how he could further help the leaders of the Revolution.

The warmth of the little man toward Villa was unmistakable—not only in his words, but in his whole attitude. "Pancho!" he said. "You're only a boy! I expected an old man!"

Pancho was almost overwhelmed. "He may look little," he thought "but he's got a big soul!" If all the rich and powerful in Mexico were like him, he told himself, there wouldn't be any need for fighting.

"How many men have you?" Madero was asking him.

"Seven hundred, *señor Presidente*—and badly armed," said Villa. He was worried about them. San Andrés was far too close to Chihuahua for comfort, he explained; and he didn't want his troops to be surprised by the *Federales* without him there to direct them. He should get back as soon as possible . . .

Madero agreed, and suggested that he visit San Andrés by train tomorrow. They parted with a warm *abrazo*, and Villa sped back to San Andrés, anxious to give Madero the kind of welcome he thought his leader deserved.

Thus it was that when Madero stepped off the train at San Andrés next day, Villa's motley cavalry was arranged in formation on either side of the street all the way from the station to the center of town; and as they saw Madero they yelled out their enthusiasm: "V*iva* Madero! V*iva* the leader of democracy! V*iva* liberty—down with dictatorship!"

Once more Madero overwhelmed Villa by taking him up into his buggy, and keeping him at his side while they moved in review along the double file of horsemen. At mealtime, he insisted Villa sit near him. Villa was used to getting the attention of rich men only over the sights of a pistol; this display of affection and respect from Madero was hard to believe.

Later, when Madero spoke to the soldiers from the bandstand in the town plaza, Villa listened, deeply moved. "Hearing him," he wrote in his memoirs several years later, "I understood how this man was able to command and guide us; and why every Revolutionary was determined to triumph or die for him!"

There was a second conference in Bustillos the following day, this one including the former wagon master Pascual Orozco. In the course of it, Madero revealed what had been on his mind since he first sent for them: What did they think of an attack on the city of Chihuahua?

Villa was against it. He remembered all too well his own defeat there, and knew the difficulties such an attack presented. They had too little ammunition, he said. The men were brave, but no matter how brave they were, they'd be lost if their ammunition gave out. "In my humble opinion," he said, and the word "humble" was said in all sincerity, "we ought to go on doing what we're doing now—fighting a guerrilla war. And we should keep trying to move north, toward the border, where we can lay our hands on more ammunition . . ."

Accordingly, within a couple of days, Villa found himself in possession of two trains which Madero had sent him. Into boxcars he loaded cannon, horses, soldiers; and by trial and error learned about trains what he had been born knowing about horses: the limits to how much they could carry, especially uphill; how gloriously they could go when the road was level or downhill; what was needed in the way of fuel or water . . .

Trains would, in time, so improve the strength and speed of Villa's army that he would come to depend on them almost utterly. But for the moment, they were a means of fulfilling Madero's orders: to make rapid and unexpected strikes at towns along the northwest rail line, as he and his men rolled north toward Ciudad Juárez.

En route, Villa paused to help Orozco in a fight for the railroad town of Bauche. They were successful, and pressed on, to meet other detachments of the army at an *hacienda* west of Ciudad Juárez, near the Rio Grande. The day following, Madero marched in at the head of his own troops —dusty, tired, wrapped in a striped *serape*—looking like a small but valiant David out to slay Goliath.

From the *hacienda*, the various detachments moved onto the outskirts of Ciudad Juárez, stationing themselves at key points just beyond the city's limits; and Madero sent a message in to General Juan Navarro of the federal army, ordering him to surrender.

Navarro was a seasoned old fighter whom Pancho had met

in battle twice before: at Chihuahua and at Cerro Prieto. Both times Navarro had defeated Villa, and after the rout at Cerro Prieto, had ordered the killing not only of prisoners but of civilian sympathizers as well. Now, stationed inside the well-fortified city, he knew his own strength. He had the river, with its customs house and its bridge to El Paso, at his back. The countryside surrounding the city was made up of low hills and open plains, reducing the possibility of surprise and giving him an easy count of Madero's troops. They numbered a scant three thousand or so—substantially fewer than his own. His answer to Madero's challenge was a flat refusal.

But before Madero's army could mount an attack, word reached both armies. There was to be no attack. An armistice had been declared.

CHAPTER 9

DURING THE WEEKS prior to the arrival of the Revolutionary army at Ciudad Juárez, outbreaks of violence had occurred all over the country. A man far more radical than Madero, Ricardo Flores Magón, had sparked revolts in Baja California, Sonora, and Veracruz. There were raids on Zacatecas by a courageous rebel named Luis Moya. And in the green and fertile valley of Morelos, a few hours south of Mexico City, a mustachio-ed young *campesino* named Emiliano Zapata was making raids on *haciendas* and burning them to the ground.

Díaz could hardly understand or accept what was happening to the country that had been so docile under his leadership for so many years. But his chief minister, the *científico* don José Limantour, who had been visiting in France, heard there enough news to know that the situation at home was serious indeed. Stopping in New York en route to Veracruz, he held consultations with Madero's provisional Vice-President, Dr. Francisco Vásquez Gómez; with Mexico's ambassador to Washington; and with members of Madero's family. It looked as though certain compromises could be arrived at, which might spare a good deal of bloodshed.

Limantour continued his journey home and began, smoothly, to pave the way toward a peaceful settlement.

Francisco Madero, who had been opposed to violence in the first place, was more than willing to agree to an armistice.

But not Pancho Villa.

He kept his feelings to himself, but this sudden halt to the fighting made him edgy and hot-tempered. Technically, his task was to keep the various segments of the army supplied with flour and coffee, sugar, corn, and cattle from Bauche and the surrounding countryside. It involved a little action, but not enough. In no time he had managed to get embroiled in a near-battle with Giuseppe Garibaldi, grandson of the famous Italian liberator. The younger Garibaldi, whom Villa referred to scornfully as a *"filibustero"*—a buccaneer—had disarmed one of Villa's soldiers who had been passing through his camp. Villa, furious at the affront, invaded Garibaldi's camp with thirty of his men, and disarmed a hundred of Garibaldi's.

When the news reached Madero, he ordered the two men to make peace. Villa swallowed his rage; and under the stern eye of his chief, gave the Italian a lukewarm *abrazo*. It did not help his temper.

As the armistice was extended, he chafed. He and Pascual Orozco felt it was shameless for the Revolutionary army to sit outside the city doing nothing. The *Federales* would think they were cowards . . .

At last, unable to contain himself any longer, he sought out Orozco privately, and suggested an idea he'd been mulling over. Suppose a few of their men were sent downstream, he said, to lure some of the federal soldiers out from cover—and then provoke them into an exchange of gunfire. "Then," he said, warming to the subject, "hearing the shots, and pretending we don't know what they are, we'd send a few more men to find out what was going on—but actually, to

The Molding of a Soldier

help the others. Then the *Federales* would have to send out more of *their* men . . . And little by little, it would get to the point where we couldn't control our men at all, they'd be so hot to charge in and attack the city. And we could prove to the President that there was nothing else to do!"

Orozco thought it was a good idea.

However, they didn't want anyone to suspect that they were the authors of the stratagem. So, after making the necessary arrangements with fifteen of their soldiers, they crossed the river upstream and made their way to El Paso, where they checked into a hotel, and went out to dinner.

The following day, hearing gunfire from the Mexican side of the river, they made a show of asking what was going on. On being told, they rented a car and headed at top speed across the bridge toward the encampments on the other side. They sought out Madero and asked, all innocence, what was happening.

"What had to happen!" said the President bitterly, and ordered them to get to their troops immediately and call a halt to the shooting. Villa and Orozco obligingly sent off fifty men to join the fifteen who were already fighting.

In a short time Madero came to Villa's headquarters and asked why the shooting was still going on.

"The men are too scattered," said Villa. "And the gunfire is too heavy for us to round them up."

"Well—go see what's happening; but get those men out of there!"

Villa and Orozco promised to send more men, to round up the combatants. But these men, too, joined the fight.

Evening was falling. Trajectories of bullets made red traces against the twilight sky. Madero came back, now thoroughly angry. "Well, how about it?" he demanded. "Are those men pulling out of there or not?"

"*Señor Presidente*," said Villa, "it's impossible to pull them out now. The men are too excited. All they want to do is fight; it's too much of a risk to hold them back. The only thing we can do now is attack the town, or let those fellows who are fighting out there get killed. And if we did that, we'd earn the resentment of the whole army, for our cowardice!"

Madero wavered a few moments. Villa understood why. Not because he lacked courage; but because he felt so deeply his responsibility for his soldiers and for the future of the Revolution. But at last he gave the two men the chance they'd been waiting for. "Well," he said reluctantly, "if that's the way it is—what do we do about it?"

Villa and Orozco told him.

Sometimes, Villa wrote in his memoirs later, a commander who was not a military man could not see what was perfectly plain to his military subordinates. And then, for the good of the campaign—especially in revolution—the subordinates must heed their own judgment, and take matters into their own hands.

It was, perhaps, a foolhardy plan. The attack involved less than a third of the Revolutionary soldiers. And, between them, Villa and Orozco had exactly two pieces of artillery: one a cannon the rebels themselves had made; and the other a small brass cannon, a veteran of the Mexican-American war of sixty years ago, which some enterprising rebel had stolen from the lawn of the El Paso City Hall.

In addition, United States troops were poised on the other side of the river, and the commander of the U. S. Fourth Cavalry had warned both Madero and Navarro of immediate intervention if any stray shells fell on Texas soil.

Nevertheless, Pascual Orozco proceeded with his plan to move along the riverside from the west, and attack the Juárez customs house. Another detachment of two hundred men would attack from the east; and Villa, with five hundred men, would attack from the railroad yards and station, at the south end of the city.

The Molding of a Soldier

He spent the night with his troops on a hill above the cemetery. Before dawn he roused them, and at four o'clock, still well before sunup, he had them on the move, down toward the railroad tracks and warehouses.

As they moved into the quiet and seemingly unoccupied area, a voice rang out: *"Quien vive?"*—"Who goes there?"— and abruptly, from all sides, came machine-gun fire: from a warehouse, from a corral, and from behind piled-up girders and sandbags that had been used to blockade the nearest streets.

Some of Villa's men fell. Others scattered. Villa drew them back to the shelter of the station house. There, he found piles of railroad ties, of which he and his men made their own barricades, and began to return the fire.

The shooting went on all day, on all sides of the city. To the north, across the river, El Paso was in an uproar. In spite of official warnings, a few stray shells did fall on Texas soil, causing some casualties. Undaunted, other Texans swarmed onto the international bridge, or climbed onto the top of boxcars and watched the excitement through binoculars. From rebel headquarters outside Ciudad Juárez, Madero sent out a volley of orders—first for a cease-fire, then to continue the attack, then for a cease-fire again. But regardless of his orders, a third of his army was on the move, and would not be turned back.

By nightfall, Villa had control of the warehouses, and pressed on to take the corral. From there, he and his men began to force entry to the streets leading into town.

The federal troops fell back before them, and Villa's men pushed ahead, moving from one protecting wall to the next, from one house to the next. All night it went on: bullets ricocheting off walls, and the muffled boom and clump of falling masonry as Villa's men dynamited houses in their way.

By morning the *Federales* broke, and fled in disarray, leaving behind the prisoners they'd taken the previous day. Villa's men flooded in to take over the abandoned positions—until, of a sudden, they were halted.

Under the command of old Juan Navarro himself, a strong column of federal footsoldiers and dragoons, armed with mortars and machine guns, had moved out of the central plaza toward the attacking troops.

Villa's advance was stopped. But not for long. His men continued to attack, from every side street and alleyway, from every doorway and window, until at last Navarro's defenses broke, and he led an orderly retreat back to the sanctuary of general headquarters. Villa's men, cheering, took over the central plaza.

Villa was well aware that the federal troops, in their defense of the town, had fought merely under orders, and hence without spirit. His own men, on the other hand, had fought with passion, for a cause they believed in; and therefore, had fought better. He was gratified, then, but not surprised, when at midafternoon on that same day—May 10th, 1911—Navarro surrendered the city to the Revolutionary army.

CHAPTER 10

IT WAS WITH forgivable pride that Villa went himself to report his victory to Madero. He then busied himself with the myriad tasks of the conqueror: taking charge of the arms and ammunition of the enemy; finding quarters for his men, and making sure they stayed sober; seeking out, with a few helpers, bodies of soldiers amid the rubble of blasted buildings, and putting them on the dead cart to be carried up to the cemetery, where still others of his men were digging a mass grave.

In the evening he went to the baker, and ordered as much bread as the man could bake by dawn. At five the next morning he came for it, and carried it still hot to the jail, knowing how low the prisoners' spirits would be after their defeat of yesterday, and how much they would depend on small comforts.

When morning was full, he returned to the barracks where Navarro and other federal officers were being held. Still elated by his triumph, he gave Navarro a big *abrazo*, to show there were no hard feelings, and an invitation to lunch in El Paso. A victor could afford to be generous!

Unfortunately, not all the rebel leaders were so euphoric.

On Villa's return from El Paso, Pascual rode up to his headquarters and dismounted, clearly angry about something. He reminded Villa that only a few short weeks ago, at Cerro Prieto, Navarro had put his prisoners before a firing squad. Surely such a man deserved the same treatment! Villa admitted that in the flush of victory, he had forgotten. Orozco pushed further. They should go to *el Presidente* tomorrow, he said, and insist that Navarro be turned over to them for execution!

Villa felt no particular bitterness toward Navarro, but found himself trapped by Orozco's logic, and was forced to agree. Accordingly, next day, he and fifty of his men met Orozco and his troops outside Madero's headquarters. Orozco, it was decided, would go inside and present their demand. "But if he refuses," said Orozco, "it's up to you to disarm Madero's guard!"

He disappeared, and Villa waited outside, uneasily.

What he could not know until later was that inside, Orozco had drawn his pistol on his commander and demanded that Navarro be delivered to him. The President had refused, and one of his brothers and don Abraham González had thrown themselves on Orozco, who had wrenched himself free and made for the door.

Villa, outside, saw Orozco and Madero reach the door almost simultaneously. Orozco, sighting Villa, shouted, "Disarm them!"

Villa—having given his word—had no choice. As he began his unhappy task, Madero saw him, and deeply hurt, said, "What's this, Pancho? Are you against me too?" He made for his automobile, parked nearby, and climbed onto the rear seat, to shout to his troops: ". . . Orozco has been deceived! I hold no rancor toward him . . . I invite him to continue to fight under my government!" And as proof, he held out his hand to the dissatisfied chieftain.

Orozco, pistol still in his right hand, did not take it.

The Molding of a Soldier

Madero turned from him and went on to the soldiers in his intense, high-pitched voice: "Here I am. Kill me if you wish. You're either with me or with Orozco. Who is the President of the Republic?"

Someone cried out, "*Viva* Madero!"

The cry swept the ranks. Now, confused, thwarted, Orozco took Madero's extended hand. Villa, overwhelmed with emotion, pushed his way past the excited soldiers to the President's car. "Shoot me!" he cried to Madero. "Punish me!"

Madero smiled and said, "Why shoot a brave man?" He told Villa to go back and quiet his troops, so they'd be in shape to continue the fight.

Sheepishly, Villa returned the confiscated rifles to Madero's guard, and went back to his own quarters to wait for Orozco to come and tell him what had happened.

There was no word from Orozco, but a rumor reached Villa which further dismayed him. Orozco, it was said, had been bribed by agents of Porfirio Díaz to make an attempt on Madero's life. He had almost succeeded in making Villa a party to his plan, but at the last moment, apparently, had lost his nerve. Hearing this, Villa could only brood on the terrible act he had so nearly been drawn into.

At the end of three days, Raul Madero came to Villa's encampment and asked why he hadn't gone to see his brother. "What do you mean, *why!*" cried Villa. "Because I'm ashamed. Don't you realize the crime Pascual Orozco was going to commit—and how I almost helped him do it?"

But no one doubted Pancho's innocence, said Raul. At that, Pancho Villa, gunman, cattle rustler, and hotheaded revolutionary, burst into tears, and Raul with him.

Together, they went to Madero's quarters. The provisional President met them, took Pancho's arm, and said, "Do you have something to say to me, Pancho?"

"I want to be relieved of my command, *señor Presidente*," said Pancho. "I'm sorry. And—I'm ashamed."

With gentle tact, Madero suggested they place Raul Madero in command of Villa's troops. Villa agreed. Madero offered him twenty-five thousand pesos, to get himself started in some sort of business. Villa refused. He had not fought the Revolution for any personal gain, he said, but for the good of the people. Madero said he was aware of this—but urged him, in any case, to take at least some of the money and any train he chose.

And then they said goodbye.

Pounding down from the north, Villa's train headed toward San Andrés. It was loaded with corn for the war widows and others of the area who had suffered serious privation during the fighting. When he reached the little town, he distributed the corn, made his official report on its distribution to Chihuahua's new governor, don Abraham González, and then settled down to busy himself at his own affairs. Now he was a civilian again, there was time to enjoy himself. There was even time to get married . . .

The first three weeks of that May, 1911, saw the success of many uprisings throughout Mexico. The capital city of Durango fell to the rebels, and Hermosillo, the capital of Sonora. In Baja California, Ricardo Flores Magón and his brother Enrique, the most radical of the Revolutionaries, had taken Tijuana and were moving down the Pacific coast toward Ensenada, while in the torrid state of Guerrero, Indians armed with machetes had risen and were on the march. Just south of Mexico City, in the lovely state of Morelos, Emiliano Zapata and his band of sombrero-ed, cartridge-belted *campesinos* had taken Cuautla.

On May 21, the wealthy resort town of Cuernavaca also fell to Zapata; but it was a victory hardly noted, in the

The Molding of a Soldier

nationwide excitement over what was happening that day in Ciudad Juárez. Representatives of the Díaz government and the Madero forces were meeting to arrange a peace.

That night, just outside the edges of the city, spokesmen for both groups met in the open, around a table illumined by automobile headlights, and signed the agreement that would disband the Revolutionary army, end the rule of Porfirio Díaz, and, pending national elections, give the interim presidency to a man equally trusted by both sides, a diplomat named Francisco León de la Barra.

It took another riot in Mexico City to persuade the ill and aging don Porfirio to draft, and sign, his resignation. But at last, at two o'clock on the morning of May 26th, he and doña Carmencita and their entourage slipped out of their quarters and into limousines waiting to take them to the railroad station.

The train took them, via tracks which had been built on order of Benito Juárez forty years ago, to the harbor of Veracruz, where they boarded a German ship anchored in the harbor. Among others, the *Federales'* General Victoriano Huerta was there to say goodbye to his commander in chief.

Ten years before, Huerta had quelled the revolt of the Mayas, in Yucatán. He was a tough, and tough-minded, Indian, stubborn and inscrutable. His heavy drinking did not keep him from being a skillful soldier; nor did it, on this quiet dawn in the Veracruz harbor, keep him from hearing and taking careful note of what old don Porfirio was saying.

"Now they will be convinced," said the old man, "by hard experience, that the only way to govern the country well is the way I did it!"

Then it was departure time, and Huerta and his men returned to shore. The ship slowly began to move. For Díaz, this moment was the end of a lifetime; he would spend the few years remaining to him in exile; he would die in Paris.

For the *Maderistas*, in their various corners of Mexico,

this quiet dawn was the consummation of all they had been fighting for.

And for Huerta, standing on the docks as the sun rose and the harborside began to come to life—for Huerta, ambitious and absolutely ruthless, this was only a beginning.

PART THREE

Betrayals

CHAPTER 11

JUST BEFORE DAWN on June 7th, 1911, the day that Madero was scheduled to arrive in the nation's capital, Mexico City was shaken by a severe earthquake. There was a sound as of a terrible storm at sea. Walls fell; buildings crumbled. More than two hundred people died under falling masonry.

For the superstitious, the event took on a special significance. It was a sign, they said, that Madero's arrival was a national catastrophe. Others insisted it signaled the end of the old, the beginning of a great new era.

Madero's arrival was delayed while damage to the railway station was repaired. However, by midafternoon, he was driven down the Paseo de la Reforma, past a crowd which cheered him from the streets, from roofs of houses, from trees—some enthusiasts even clinging to statues along the way. When he reached the Zócalo, the city's vast central plaza which had once been the site of Aztec pyramids and a great sacrificial stone, a mob was waiting there too, to greet him with shouts of "Viva Madero!" and "Viva la democracia!" Later, when he emerged from the National Palace after his meeting with interim President Francisco de la Barra, the crowd was still there, sending up its fervent shouts: *Viva la libertad!*"

It seemed, at first, that liberty was indeed in the making. Elections would be held in October—the first free elections since the time of Benito Juárez. An amnesty was declared, freeing political prisoners from their cells in the Belém penitentiary, and from their dank underground holds in the island fortress of San Juan de Ulúa at Veracruz. There were to be no more restrictions on the press; and workers were free to organize trade unions.

For some, however, it was a hollow freedom. Emiliano Zapata came to the capital for lunch and an interview with Madero. It was Zapata who had taken Cuautla and Cuernavaca from the *Federales*, and seized and burned *haciendas* all over the state of Morelos. Now, he wanted to know about the land which had been taken from the peasants during Díaz's regime—land which had been theirs since the earliest Spanish land grants. When would it be returned?

Zapata was a slight young man, with dark eyes and a drooping black mustache. When he was a child, the village where his family lived had been destroyed to make room for an *hacienda*, its orchards ripped up to be replaced by fields of sugar cane. Zapata had been only eight when it had happened, but he remembered all his life the sight of his father weeping helplessly at the outrage.

Grown to adulthood, he had tried to help his fellow villagers regain, by legal means, their own and the public land which had been taken from them. But their claims were rejected summarily; and they were warned by the new landowners that if they so much as set foot on the land, they would be shot. It was small wonder that when they heard about Madero and his revolution, they took up arms; and aided by peasants from all over the state, followed Zapata to vent their anger and bitterness against the *hacendados* who had robbed them.

Betrayals

Now the Revolutionaries had defeated the *Porfiristas*—but not a square meter of land had been returned. Instead, President de la Barra had sent troops into Morelos, trying to arrest Zapata and disband his army. What kind of revolution was this?

The peasant leader sat at lunch, shy, distrustful, clutching his pistol all through the meal, and posed the question. He asked Madero to stop the government's persecution of his men. And he asked for a return of the peasant lands—soon. His men were armed, he said, and they were impatient.

Madero, however, made no promises. He said only that all would be taken care of "in time." And Zapata—thoroughly dissatisfied, but willing to keep his men in check for a brief while longer—went back to Morelos.

The interview should have been a warning to Madero that men who had fought for land would not accept words instead. But Madero did not understand the urgency. He had never known poverty, or hunger. For him, political freedom was the first order of business. Land, and bread, could wait.

Actually, it was his desire for a peaceful transition from Díaz's regime to his own, and his fear of radical change, which would bring about his own tragic end and precipitate a much more savage war than that which had just been fought. He kept in office the same body of government employees that Díaz had left behind; and, for the most part, chose to maintain the existing structure of the army, under the same officers.

Hence, all the while he was attempting to make peace with Zapata, two *Porfirista* army chiefs, Aureliano Blanquet and Victoriano Huerta, were pressing campaigns against the peasant guerrillas. Madero seemed unwilling, or unable, to control his generals. By November, soon after Madero was sworn into the presidency, Zapata publically denounced him, and declared for his own "Plan"—the "Plan of Ayala," asking for immediate distribution to the peasants of one-third of all *hacienda* land.

There were others, too, who felt that Madero had no program. His former provisional Vice-President, Dr. Francisco Vásquez Gómez, who had helped prepare the peace treaty, turned from him in disillusion. There was fighting in the Tehuantepec isthmus and in the southeast, and in Oaxaca too. A former governor of Nuevo León, Bernardo Reyes, tried to "declare" for a government of his own, but found no followers. The United States ambassador, Henry Lane Wilson —who was bitterly anti-Madero in any case—reported home that Mexico was "seething with discontent."

But it was news of a rash of small revolts in the north which most disturbed Madero. After all, the northerners were the men who had been his companions-in-arms during the fighting at Casas Grandes and Ciudad Juárez. To learn the facts of the matter, he sent off to Chihuahua for the one man he thought he could trust.

For the last half year, Pancho Villa had been living quietly with his wife Luz in a little house on Tenth Street, and his business as butcher and slaughterhouse owner was thriving. But when Madero's message came, near the close of 1911, he went immediately to Mexico City, and there was given an invitation to lunch with the President at Chapultepec Castle.

To a rough-and-tumble *campesino* like Villa, the castle was an awesome place. Built on a hillside in the park, it was a great battlemented structure which had once housed the national school of cadets, and later had been turned into an exquisite dwelling by the Emperor Maximilian and his wife. Outside were shaded promenades that looked down over a sea of treetops and across myriad rooftops toward the two great

Betrayals 69

volcanic peaks that dominated the valley of Mexico. Inside, the furnishings ranged from the Louis XV salons of the puppet emperor, to the mid-Victorian mahogany of don Porfirio and his Carmencita. It was in the great formal dining room that Madero talked with Villa over *comida*, the midday meal.

Once more, Villa was overwhelmed by the warmth and respect Madero showed him. This was a man he would die for, if need be.

"Pancho," said the President, "I sent for you to tell me what's happening with Pascual Orozco. I hear unpleasant things about him."

Villa told him as much as he knew: that Orozco spent much of his time these days with the two richest cattle barons in Chihuahua—one of them Alberto Terrazas, a man whom Orozco, less than a year ago, had hated as a tyrant and oppressor.

Madero was silent; then, "Listen, Pancho," he said. "If Orozco betrays the Revolution, will you be loyal to my government?"

"Yes, *señor Presidente*," Villa answered promptly. "With my whole heart."

Madero smiled and took his hand. "That's what I hoped you'd say. Go back to Chihuahua, and keep your eyes on Orozco. And let me know what happens."

The rumors about Orozco were quite true. After the victory of the Revolutionaries, Orozco had wanted a big cash prize, but had received only a small one. He had wanted to be named to Madero's cabinet, but instead had merely been appointed chief of the northern military zone. Now, his discontent known, he was being cultivated by the Terrazas family, whose blandishments fell on fertile soil.

Orozco's opening gambit against Madero's government came early in February 1912. By a ruse, he tried to lure

Villa into an attack on the Chihuahua penitentiary, and sent men and ammunition to help him in the attempt.

But Villa saw through the plan, and sent Orozco a message in answer. "Señor Orozco," it read, ". . . I am not totally without shame. I leave you your soldiers. I am going back to the desert to prove that I am a man of honor." He chose eleven workers from his slaughterhouse, equipped them, and set out with them for the dry southern plains of Chihuahua to seek recruits for what he knew would be a battle against his former comrade.

Men poured off the *ranchos* to join him, and in a short time he had a group of five hundred, gathered from Satevó, Ciénega de Ortiz, and elsewhere—most of them already armed and mounted.

He and his followers were camped at an *hacienda*, awaiting Orozco's next move, when, late one cold afternoon, an automobile drove up, and Pascual Orozco's father dismounted, asking to speak to Villa privately.

When they were alone, Orozco senior told Pancho how much his son Pascual had always admired him. And on behalf of himself and his son, he offered Villa three hundred thousand pesos to withdraw to the United States—or, if he preferred, to stay in Chihuahua but to refrain from interfering in Orozco's future plans.

Villa heard him out. Finally, "The government of señor Madero," he said, "was created by the people, and we gave it our approval, you and I . . . Tell your son he can't buy me, no matter how much he offers. And say that though we used to be friends, from now on we're going to be trading bullets." He enlarged on the denunciation a moment or two, and then closed the discussion.

Orozco senior turned to leave. But by now it was snowing, and he had no overcoat. Villa took off his *serape*, and gave it to the older man. He stood watching for a long time, till the

Betrayals 71

car was out of sight. It must be, he thought, the worst fate in the world to be the father of a traitor.

But—perhaps the months of peace had left Villa rusty in his old guerrilla skills. More likely, the political confusion in Chihuahua left the battle lines unclear in the minds of the people. For whatever reason, Villa's first few skirmishes were unsuccessful and desertions depleted his ranks. He was able to get control of the garrison at Parral, and for a few days, the city was his. But he was set upon by fifteen hundred *Orozquista* reinforcements, and after a hard fight, was driven out, losing much of his equipment. Most of his forces were still intact, however, and were able to move on toward Torreón, headquarters for the government's northern division.

Madero's General González Salas suffered a much greater defeat, in a pivotal battle on the plains of southern Chihuahua. Orozco's *Colorados*—his "red-flaggers," experienced and hard-riding—had run roughshod over the government troops; there had been heavy casualties. Salas, en route by train to Torreón, exhausted, wounded, and disgraced, put an end to his life.

The situation in the north seemed perilous. Madero's cabinet, alarmed by the daily arrival in Mexico City of trainloads of wounded, pressed Madero to appoint a strong new chief for the northern armies. Reluctantly, Madero appointed the man of their choice: hard-drinking, inscrutable, ambitious Victoriano Huerta, and sent him to Torreón to assume command.

CHAPTER 12

VILLA HAD BEEN requested, in a wire from Madero, to place himself and his men under the command of General Huerta. Though he had already worked out plans of his own to rid the area of Orozco's rebels, he reported dutifully to the general at Torreón, that April of 1912, and his first two interviews with the tough old Indian went smoothly enough. Huerta seemed cordial, and at Villa's request, agreed to replace the guerrilla unit's old .30-.30s with Mausers. Their third interview, however, was more troubling to Villa. The old chief, thoroughly drunk, called for him one hot, dry day, and ordered him to leave then and there for an attack on the *Orozquistas* at Tlahualilo.

Pancho tried to protest; but Huerta said angrily, "I order you to march immediately!"

An attack at midafternoon, Pancho knew, could be fatal; the dust his cavalry would kick up would telegraph their approach for miles. However, he found a general who would explain his case to Huerta, waited till evening, then undertook the march under cover of night.

This time, he was in charge not only of his own men, but of the division's Seventh Cavalry as well; and as he neared

Betrayals 73

Tlahualilo—barely visible as a patch of deeper darkness in the dark distance—he was painfully aware of his lack of orthodox military experience. But he reminded himself that a successful commander laid his plans well in advance, and then hewed to them. Accordingly, he left the dark open plain and moved into the chaparral, bypassing the *Orozquista* advance lines, and, at the first light of dawn, attacked from the flank.

For five or six hours there was heavy fighting; but by the time one of his artillery commanders arrived with cannon, the enemy was already in retreat. Villa's spoils, in that brief morning's engagement, consisted of saddles, rifles, ammunition, ten carloads of food, and more than six hundred horses.

The dust of the north-central deserts was at once his friend and his enemy. It could betray his approach; or, as he learned from Colonel Rubio Navarrete during an attack a few days later, it could conceal from the enemy the fact that he had no infantry—if, of course, his men approached at a gallop and kicked up enough sand. Navarrete, a brilliant artilleryman, taught Villa many things that would prove useful to him; and Villa acquired a profound respect for him.

During his first few weeks under Huerta, he was appointed brigadier general. It was an honor he didn't want; he was afraid his men would laugh at him. However, he reminded himself that he was fighting for the good of the people, and if his being a brigadier would help, well—so be it!

So it was as a brigadier that he moved, with Navarrete's artillery immediately behind him, toward the enemy at Sierra de Conejos, on the way north toward Parral and Chihuahua. As they advanced, Navarrete's cannonballs whistled so low over the heads of Villa's cavalrymen that they were terrified. Time and again Villa sent back word that the artillery were shooting too low. Each time, Navarrete answered that there was no cause for worry; the fire was well-placed. Sure enough, the shells played havoc with the enemy's front lines, breaking an opening for Villa's cavalry to penetrate. Villa's confidence in Navarrete grew—a confidence which would soon prove justified in a different sort of situation altogether.

He felt less trust, however, in Victoriano Huerta.

He never saw his chief sober—neither at seven in the morning nor at midnight. It was a source of astonishment to Villa, who could drink very little without getting sick, that Huerta's military judgment was so sound, considering his almost perpetual state of drunkenness.

But there was something else that bothered him more. Notwithstanding the praise and the *abrazos* that Huerta showered on him after a successful sortie, he sensed that the general felt no real warmth toward him; and he was aware that Huerta's army regulars treated him and his guerrilla fighters with open scorn.

He saw the most decisive evidence of this after a victorious action at Sierra de Conejos. Smallpox, typhus, and other diseases had been plaguing the *Huertista* troops; and some sort of severe illness had struck Villa in the early morning. He had fought on, however, until he saw the enemy withdraw; then, at last, had lain down on his *serape*, feverish and exhausted. Huerta's chief of staff rode up and, finding Villa shivering on the ground, ordered him on his feet to continue fighting. He refused to believe that the battle was over and that the soldiers retreating in the distance were Orozco's rebels; they were Emilio Madero's men, he said, and accused Villa of having spent the day lying there doing nothing.

Villa's answer was quick, angry, and profane, and the officer rode off, smoldering.

That night, Villa's friend Tomás Urbina—like Villa, a former outlaw—gave him an alcohol rub and wrapped him in blankets to sweat out the fever. Villa slept under a cart, afterwards, in a vain attempt to protect himself from the cold night air.

Betrayals

But by day, sick as he was, he kept to his feet, obeying Huerta's orders to the letter. He and another general took the town of Escalón, amid the dry washes and sandy wastes of southern Chihuahua. It was while they were in this area that Villa received the astonishing news that his friend Urbina had been seized by Huerta's soldiers and was now a prisoner.

Outraged, Villa marched his forces several miles away from the rest of the division, and dispatched an angry note to three of the Federalist generals, saying that if Colonel Urbina were not released immediately, he would contact the President himself.

Response was immediate. "General, don't be alarmed," read the generals' answer. "We guarantee that your *compadre* will be with you by eight in the morning. We have already discussed the matter with General Huerta."

Sure enough, Urbina was back in Villa's camp by morning. Had Villa been more schooled in intrigue, however, he might have realized that Urbina's arrest was undoubtedly an attempt by Huerta to isolate Villa from his supporters and weaken him.

But whatever his military position with Huerta, those days, his standing among the ordinary people of Chihuahua was made eminently clear when his chief ordered him into Parral, together with General Antonio Rábago, to install authorities to govern the city. Parral considered Villa one of their own. The townspeople turned out in droves to meet him; bands played in wild enthusiasm. Sprays of flowers were offered him, but Villa, already worried about the regular army's jealousy of him, urged the bearers to give their offerings to General Rábago.

His display of tact went for nothing. When he returned to division headquarters in Jiménez, he discovered that during his absence one of his mares had been appropriated by a regular army captain. He reported the matter to Huerta and asked for the animal's return. Huerta responded with an impatience, and an arrogance, that Villa found intolerable; and for a moment words flew. Then both men calmed down, and the matter was resolved with the mare's return.

It did not seem an important occurrence. But it would prove more serious than Villa knew.

In spite of medicines prescribed by the company doctor, and Urbina's alcohol rubs, Villa was still plagued by fever. The night of his return from Parral he was having a blanket sweat, when two of Huerta's officers brought him word to report to the chief. Villa, drenched in perspiration and shivering, pointed out his condition and asked to be allowed to report in the morning instead.

It was a fatal error. In the morning, wrapped in a *serape*—it was June now and the summer's torrential rains had begun—he reported to Huerta's headquarters and was told by two junior officers to hand over his arms.

Puzzled, he obeyed. He could see soldiers lining up on both sides of the railroad car Huerta used as an office. There must be some mistake, he thought. Still dizzy from the illness and the night's sweating, he followed the officers when they ordered him outside; he was marched through a double file of soldiers toward an adobe wall nearby—and abruptly, he realized that a number of the men were forming a square and that he was about to be shot.

It was unbelievable. After all his services to the Revolution! Men he had fought beside were going to execute him!

The sergeant of the firing squad moved to mark an X on the wall with his bayonet and ordered Villa to stand in front of it. Villa turned incredulously to the colonel who had escorted him out here.

"Señor Colonel, will you tell me why you're going to shoot me? If I have to die, at least I want to know why. I've been

Betrayals

a loyal servant of the government. I've worked beside you. I've run risks. It's only fair to tell me why I'm facing a firing squad!"

By now he was crying in rage against such injustice. The colonel, O'Horgan, said nothing. Villa turned to the second officer, Colonel Castro. "Señor Colonel, I give you my last *abrazo*. The army, if it has any honor, will judge this act. I'm innocent!"

Moved, upset, Castro returned Villa's embrace. All he could say was, "It's an order . . ."

Abruptly, O'Horgan said, "Wait a minute, *compañero*. Don't shoot him yet. Wait till I've talked to General Huerta."

He disappeared. In a moment he was back, saying helplessly, "General Huerta says to comply with the order."

Once more the sergeant ordered Villa to take his place against the wall. Villa again protested, begging to know the reason he had been condemned. The sergeant, impatient to get on with the execution, shoved Villa toward the wall, and Villa—hoping someone, *any*one, would come to his aid—fell to the ground as if the push had knocked him down. At this moment the colonel of artillery, Rubio Navarrete, appeared and took in the situation. He insisted that the squad hold their fire while he went back to make his own appeal to Huerta.

Villa was sure it would be a futile attempt. He emptied his pockets, giving his watch to one of the men on the firing squad and such cash as he had with him to the others.

Finally Navarrete reappeared. "The execution is suspended. On order of the general."

But all Huerta himself would say, when Villa was escorted before him, was: "My honor as an officer was at stake." There was no other word of explanation.

Apparently, however, Huerta felt it wiser not to let Villa return among his men even for a moment. They were allowed to assemble outside the train, and the prisoner was permitted to say a few words of goodbye to them from the platform. But even those few words roused such an emotion in them that he was quickly ordered inside, out of sight. Just before the train pulled out, he arranged for Navarrete to be given his horse, his saddle, and his sword in gratitude.

And then the train was on its way eastward, and then to the south. During the four days' journey Villa recognized the station at Torreón, then Monterrey, then San Luis Potosí . . . At last, in the small hours of the night, they reached the capital.

The last time he had been here, he had come at the President's invitation. This time, he was hustled at gunpoint through the dark streets from the station to the federal penitentiary.

Twelve days later, he discovered what the charges against him were. A young officer of the army's advocate general's office told him he had been accused of threatening to throw his troops against the federal army—this, perhaps, referring to Villa's actions after his friend Urbina's arrest near Escalón. He was also accused of "sacking the town of Parral," of disobedience and insubordination.

Villa clarified the first charge. Regarding the second, the "sacking" of Parral—to be sure, when he had first taken Parral during his independent campaign against Orozco, he had exacted a forced loan from Parral's bankers and businessmen, to pay and feed his troops. But, as he pointed out to the young officer, the "loan" he had exacted was in lieu of money Madero had already promised him for the costs of his campaign. Far from sacking the town, he had kept his soldiers in firm check, and the ordinary townspeople had felt nothing but gratitude and affection for him.

As for the charge of insubordination—well, he and Huerta,

Betrayals

he admitted, had sometimes exchanged a few hot words. But never had he refused to carry out a military order.

It took four months to clear him of the Parral charges. During much of this time, he was held incommunicado. It was fortunate, during those lonely months, that on his compaigns he had learned to read a little; because his only distraction, in the penitentiary, was struggling through a copy of *The Three Musketeers* which a young judge had brought him.

In due time, he was transferred to the military prison Santiago Tlaltelolco. The rules for his solitary confinement were relaxed, and he was allowed to speak occasionally to other prisoners. One was General Bernardo Reyes, in jail because of his attempted rebellion against Madero earlier in the year.

Another privilege granted him was one enjoyed by the lowliest felon in a Mexican jail—the "connubial visit." This meant he was allowed a few hours alone, once a week, with the woman of his choice.

His wife Luz remained in the north, in San Andrés; but his marriage had never kept him from enjoying other women during his campaigns, and it did not limit him now. An attractive girl named Rosita Palacios came to him each week in the prison, and her visits did much to make his sentence bearable.

CHAPTER 13

THE YEAR WAS wearing away. Villa's last hope was to write Madero about Huerta's charges, explaining what had really happened. But Madero's answer, when it came, made it clear he believed Huerta's version of the story. For Villa, this was the ultimate heartbreak.

But however discouraged he felt at Madero's rejection, he could not stay inactive long. Some germ of optimism told him that perhaps some day he would be back at his slaughterhouse, and that once there it would be helpful to know how to typewrite and keep books. Accordingly, he got permission to go to the courtroom daily, when court was not in session, and practice on the typewriter there.

He shared use of the machine with a poverty-stricken young court clerk named Carlos Jáuregui, who felt a deep sympathy with the caged guerrilla fighter; and before long, a friendship had sprung up between them. It was Jáuregui who told him he might be in serious danger from his enemies and advised him to try to escape.

It was Jáuregui, too, who evolved the safest method of escape. They should file through the bars of the gate separating the prison chambers from the courtyard and exterior

Betrayals 81

offices, he suggested. From there, in suitable disguise, Villa could leave the prison openly, by the main entrance.

The notion of disguise delighted Villa. "Good! I'll be the lawyer don Jesús José Martínez. How does it sound?"

Jáuregui liked it. With Villa's money, he bought respectable clothing of the sort a lawyer might wear and a pair of pistols. The day he brought the purchases to Villa's quarters, however, Villa was assailed by sudden doubts. "Remember, boy," he warned. "If you make one false move, you'll be the first one I shoot!"

"If there is treachery, my general," said Jáuregui, "you'll have plenty of reason to kill me."

The most troublesome problem was with the courtroom gate. The rasp of the file on the iron bars made a noise that could be heard all down the corridor. This they solved, at length, by doing their filing when the army band was playing *ranchero* music for the inmates and guards. Not only were the halls emptied then, but the rasp of the file was overwhelmed by the echoing blare of the brasses.

At length, everything was in readiness. They expected to make their attempt the afternoon of December 24th, "*la noche buena*," Christmas eve. But on that crucial day, Villa received a surprise visit from a lawyer friend named Antonio Tamayo, who hinted to Villa that he knew something about his escape plans.

Villa was startled. Thinking back, he realized he might have let slip a few unwise words when he had been speaking recently to his fellow prisoner General Bernardo Reyes. Tamayo, also a friend of Reyes, continued: "Pancho, I'm here to make an offer that should interest you." The Madero government, he said, could not last—nor should it. People high in government and the army were preparing its deathblow, and they wanted Pancho on their side. If he promised to support them, said Tamayo, they guaranteed he would be free in six days' time.

Pancho listened, inwardly boiling with fury at the treachery. But he kept an impassive face, and thanked Tamayo, asking for a few days to think it over.

Tamayo, sure of his cooperation, gave him an *abrazo* and went—leaving Villa once more in tears that it should be Madero's enemies who offered him liberty, while Madero, whose cause he supported with his whole heart, had kept him prisoner here and ignored his pleas.

The visit had delayed Villa's escape. Christmas Day passed; but on the afternoon of the twenty-sixth, he got himself ready. He hid the pistols under his shirt, enveloped the cartridges in his handkerchief, and wrapped himself in a *serape*, grateful that the weather was cold enough to make it seem necessary. He left his quarters, paused to chat with the young lieutenant colonel posted in an office down the corridor, strolled with him a few moments along the hallway in full sight of the guards, then excused himself to go to the courtroom.

Jáuregui was waiting for him.

With great effort, Villa managed to bend the sawed-through iron bars of the gate, leaving an opening wide enough to crawl through into the office beyond. There, Jáuregui provided him with an overcoat, a sober black hat, and a pair of dark glasses. Villa put them on. "My friend, do you really think I can pass for a lawyer?"

The clerk reassured him—but cautioned him to keep his handkerchief to his nose, as with a heavy cold. Conversing casually, they walked past various offices, until they reached the main entrance of the prison. A chauffeured automobile, by prearrangement, was waiting for them across the street; and in a moment they were wending their way through the streets of the city.

Something neither of them had expected was to be stopped

Betrayals

at a checkpoint where the road to Toluca turned off, and to be questioned by two *rurales*. Who were they? Where were they going? Did they have arms? Jáuregui and the "lawyer Martínez" got out of the car, while the *rurales* searched under the car seats for guns or ammunition. They were afraid, it seemed, that any firearms might reach the *Zapatistas* operating in the mountains of the state of Mexico, beyond the city limits.

A moment more, and the young clerk and his passenger were allowed to get back into the car and resume their way, winding along the cold, high, wooded road to Toluca.

Once there, Villa's first act was to shave off his telltale mustache. Then they rented rooms. Villa was feeling victorious at the escape, and in a mood to celebrate. "How are you with the girls, my young friend?" he asked Jáuregui.

"With the girls, General?"

"Yes, my friend, with the girls."

"I don't know, General."

"Well," said Pancho, thoroughly tired of his long imprisonment and eager for diversion, "let's go find out!"

By the following morning, the story of Villa's escape was in all the newspapers. Without wasting any more time, the clerk and the "lawyer Martínez"—whose cold by now was so severe he rarely came out from behind his handkerchief—took the train to Guadalajara, and thence to Colima. Then to sultry Manzanillo, on the Pacific, where they hoped to catch a boat going north.

Aboard the boat, Villa caught sight of a man he knew— a telegrapher for Huerta's Northern Division. Desperate, he and Jáuregui bribed the steward for a stateroom, where Villa remained hidden until they reached Mazatlán—while Jáuregui, stationed on deck to keep an eye on the telegrapher, got thoroughly seasick.

Ashore at Mazatlán they checked into a hotel, only to

discover the telegrapher had checked into the same one. The next day they found him on their train, bound for the fishing port of Guaymas—but there, at last, he went his way, without ever having recognized Villa.

The train continued north. The tracks led inland now, and it was cold. As they drew toward Nogales, there was a light snow falling. Anxious to avoid immigration difficulties at the frontier checkpoint, Villa and Jáuregui jumped off the train before it reached its destination. They sought a less conspicuous point of entry and, together, strolled casually across the international line into Arizona.

It was January 3rd, 1913. They were, for the moment, safe in the United States. But Villa was sure they would not be there long; he knew all too well the trouble that was about to break out in his homeland.

CHAPTER 14

BY THE BEGINNING of 1913, everyone in Mexico City knew that a serious blow against the Madero government was in the making and, for the most part, who was involved. Even Gustavo Madero, the President's brother, knew. But the President would not believe it.

First of all, his two most serious contenders for the presidency were in prison. General Bernardo Reyes was in the military prison of Santiago Tlaltelolco; and Felix Díaz, the soft, spoiled nephew of old don Porfirio, having attempted a coup at Veracruz the previous October, was now in the penitentiary in Mexico City. As for Pascual Orozco—he had been roundly beaten all over the state of Chihuahua and had fled across the border into the United States.

To be sure, the press, so newly freed, had kept up a steady sniping at the government, through all of 1912. Gustavo Madero said it was like "biting the hand that removed the muzzle." And Mexicans of wealth and position steadfastly boycotted the presidential receptions. But that was only to be expected . . .

There remained, of course, the problem of Emiliano Zapata and his peasant army, in Morelos and elsewhere.

Zapata had quickly lost faith in Madero's willingness to restore peasant and village lands, and had taken the offensive again, raiding and burning *haciendas* almost to the city's edge.

But during the year, Madero had done what he could, slowly, to implement his promises to the Mexican people. His battle cry, during his campaign against Porfirio Díaz, had been: "Effective suffrage, no reelection"; and he had striven to give Mexico just that. His election had been, in all likelihood, the most honest in forty years. He left the dispensing of justice to the judges; he did not force his partisans on the various states as governors; he did not execute the military chiefs who had opposed him. Instead, he had ordered the building of rural schools, and established a system of free lunches for schoolchildren. He rebuilt the war-damaged railroads. Late in the year, he even held secret meetings with Zapata in an effort to arrive at some plan for land redistribution, though it was clear the cost of such a program would be prohibitive.

But there seemed no pleasing the people. They were used to heroes, colorful and strong, and by no definition could Madero be called a hero. He was a gentle, kindly, earnest man, scrupulously honest. He strove to believe well of all human beings, even when the evidence pointed overwhelmingly to their guilt.

That, in fact, was his tragic flaw.

And he had two powerful enemies: one, Victoriano Huerta, inside his government, and the other outside it—the American ambassador, Henry Lane Wilson.

Wilson was a quick, dry, nervous man with a toupée, pince-nez glasses perched on his thin nose, and a drooping gray mustache. He was a dedicated conservative, with a deep distrust of democracy in the hands of any such "backward" nation as Mexico. Additionally, he was closely associated with American mining and smelting interests in Mexico which were in direct competition with those of the Madero family.

Betrayals

He had been a staunch supporter of the Díaz regime, which had been so generous with concessions to foreign investors. But when Madero came to office, his dispatches home began to drip with scorn. Madero, he said, was a mountebank. He had a "disorganized brain"; and the Madero government he described as corrupt, inept, and of all things, tyrannical. When he spoke to Madero at public gatherings he was condescending and insulting. At every opportunity he predicted the fall of the regime, and in fact, as matters came to a climax, did much to make his prediction come true.

During January, 1913, the conspiracy went forward. Gustavo Madero was shown a list of the conspirators, including almost every top official in the local army garrison; but when he took the list to his brother, Francisco Madero dismissed it as fraudulent. A presidential aide who also obtained evidence of the plan tried to reach Madero to warn him; was denied an audience; in desperation passed the information on to señora Madero; and incurred only the President's wrath. Even José Pino Suárez, the Vice-President, tried to convince the Secretary of War of the seriousness of the plot, but was rebuffed.

Meanwhile, the conspirators were going from officer to officer of the federal army in the capital, until they had enlisted almost the entire Twenty-ninth Battalion. One of the wealthier conspirators, Cecilio Ocón, bought a hotel just off the Zócalo, and truckloads of "construction materials" arrived daily at the site—concealing every kind of arms and ammunition. The school of cadets was alerted to be ready to move; and General Bernardo Reyes, still dreaming of the presidency from inside his prison walls, had his finest uniform in readiness.

Discovering that Gustavo Madero had become aware of their activities, the conspirators set Sunday morning, February 9th, as the day of their planned uprising. By two o'clock in the morning, soldiers at Tacubaya, a suburb on a slight rise just to the south and west of Chapultepec Park, were marching out of their barracks armed with cannon and machine guns.

It was a cold night, clear and quiet; a guard on the terrace of the presidential residence at Chapultepec Castle was alerted by sounds, and looking down past the treetops below, could make out the shadowy shapes of a large armed unit, with horse-drawn cannon, proceeding through the darkness along the avenue edging the park. He notified Gustavo Madero and the *comandante* of the National Palace.

The younger Madero went immediately to the palace, and with passionate pleas revived the loyalty of the palace guard, putting at their head the aging but still faithful General Lauro Villar.

The insurgent column had, in the meantime, divided, one part going to the military prison of Santiago Tlaltelolco to free General Bernardo Reyes, the other moving to the penitentiary to free Felix Díaz—who, not expecting their arrival so early, was halfway through shaving. He joined them as he was.

And fifteen miles from the heart of the city, the six hundred military cadets climbed aboard streetcars and traveled swiftly through the predawn dark, to rendezvous with the other conspirators at the *Zócalo*. In total, the rebel troops reaching the great central plaza numbered roughly three thousand men; the loyal troops stationed in the National Palace, about five hundred.

Bernardo Reyes, resplendent in his gold braid, rode forward to lead the charge on the palace. The palace guard opened fire, and Reyes was killed instantly.

There was heavy firing, but in the end the rebels were routed, withdrawing to the *Ciudadela*—the citadel and arsenal—leaving the loyal troops still in possession of the National Palace.

As the confusion cleared, and it was considered safe enough for the President to move out onto the streets, Madero started on horseback down the Paseo de la Reforma. Crowds had already congregated; they cheered him as he passed. En route, there was sniper fire, and Madero was persuaded to take temporary shelter in a photographer's studio. Here, by chance, he met Victoriano Huerta, who gave him an emotional *abrazo* and assured him of his support.

Madero resumed his ride to the National Palace, and there learned that a rebel bullet had seriously wounded the loyal old General Villar, leaving the government troops without a leader. The President then made a decision that would cost him his life. He appointed, as chief of the government troops—Victoriano Huerta.

That was the beginning of the *docena tragica*—the twelve tragic days. Although the government forces had seemingly won the day, the rebel troops were safely within the walls of the *Ciudadela*. And Huerta, as head of the loyal troops, began what was truly a "phony war." With a great show of activity, he dispersed his artillery so his guns could not possibly damage the *Ciudadela*; sending instead loyal cavalry and infantrymen in suicidal attacks on the rebel stronghold, to be mowed down by the hundreds.

As for the Judas kiss which he had given Madero the morning the uprisings had begun, it was only the first. He would give him, in the days that followed, several more.

The city was plunged into chaos. Garbage went uncollected. There was no electricity, and for days no foodstuffs could reach the inhabitants. Huerta's cannon were aimed anywhere but toward the rebel centers; shells fell in business and residential areas, killing hundreds of civilians. Corpses lay in the street unburied, or doused with kerosene and burned where they lay.

Shortly after it had all begun, there was a secret meeting between Felix Díaz the rebel, and Victoriano Huerta, the government's army leader. It was not so secret, however, but that Gustavo Madero got wind of it and reported it to his brother. But the President, himself incapable of treachery, could not believe it in others; and on his next meeting with Huerta, accepted another *abrazo* from him, as Huerta assured him, "You are secure in the arms of General Huerta!"

Gustavo Madero was not so gullible. Surprising Huerta after dinner one night, he took his pistol and placed him under arrest. But Huerta went next day to the President, reiterated his loyalty, was reinstated in his command, and received his pistol back from the President himself.

It would be Gustavo's last chance to try to save his brother. The afternoon of the eighteenth, Huerta arranged that he and Gustavo would both attend a luncheon at a downtown restaurant. There, a squad of soldiers seized Gustavo. At the same time, a squad of General Blanquet's soldiers—also supposedly loyal—invaded the National Palace on a pretext, shot three of Madero's supporters, and seized Madero, his Vice-President Pino Suárez, and a still-loyal general of artillery, Felipe Angeles. At that precise moment, on order of General Huerta, the bells of the great cathedral facing the *Zócalo* began to ring, signaling the end of the Madero reign.

Gustavo Madero was taken from the restaurant by automobile to the *Ciudadela* as a captive. There he was set upon by one of the conspirators—Cecilio Ocón, who had bought the hotel for use as an armory just prior to the uprising—and by a mob of rebel soldiers. He was stabbed, shot, and dismembered.

Francisco Madero, however, would last a few days longer. Huerta had other plans for him.

Because it would be well to make his own accession to the presidency look as legal as possible, Huerta notified the captive Madero that he had two choices: resign his office,

Betrayals 91

and be allowed to go into exile; or cling to it, and be killed.

Madero, dreaming that one day he could return from exile and free his country again, chose to resign. Pino Suárez, the Vice-President, did likewise.

By the time Huerta had similarly persuaded the Minister of Foreign Relations to resign, he himself became next in succession; and a confused Congress confirmed him as President.

A train was waiting at the station, to take Madero, Pino Suárez and their families to Veracruz to meet a boat for Havana and exile. But it continued to wait. Madero remained a prisoner.

And what, while this had been happening, had the American ambassador been doing?

He had known of Huerta's secret meetings with the rebel leader Felix Díaz and had given the conspiracy his approval. He had bombarded his government with false reports of Díaz's popularity with the Mexican people. He asked that President William Howard Taft send down warships, whose movements he himself should direct—though in this, at least, he was rebuffed by his State Department. And after Madero had been arrested and Felix Díaz came to the American embassy to work out plans for the country's future, he greeted Díaz with: "Long live General Díaz, the savior of Mexico!"

Another diplomat who was present at the scene asked about the fate of "poor Madero." Wilson merely shrugged. "Oh, they'll put Madero in a madhouse, where he should always be kept," he said. "As for the other [Pino Suárez], he is nothing but a scoundrel, so if they kill him it will be no great loss."

The Chilean ambassador, appalled, said, "We must not allow it!" Whereupon Wilson, who had conspired for weeks with Díaz and Reyes, countered severely, "We must not meddle in the domestic affairs of Mexico!"

The following day, he notified his government that Madero's "wicked despotism" had fallen.

On the twentieth, after appeals by the Madero family had failed, Wilson was visited at the American embassy by gallant, determined little señora Madero—who had joined her husband outside Ciudad Juárez, two years before, and had been at his side through every crisis since. She had come to ask that Wilson intercede with Huerta, to spare her husband's life.

Wilson was brusque and abrupt with her; at moments he lectured her irritably. His kindly, good-hearted wife was with him, and pulled at his coat, in an effort to persuade him to speak to the poor woman more gently.

Madero's downfall, Wilson said, was "due to the fact that he never wanted to consult with me . . . Your husband," he went on, "had peculiar ideas."

"Mr. Ambassador," señora Madero answered, "my husband had not peculiar ideas, but high ideals." She asked also that he attempt to protect the life of the Vice-President, but Wilson said impatiently that Pino Suárez was a very bad man; that he was to blame for most of Madero's troubles. "That kind of man must disappear!"

Señora Madero reminded him that Pino Suárez had a wife and six children. The ambassador merely shrugged. By the interview's end he had made vague assurances that Madero would not suffer bodily harm; but señora Madero had little faith that he would make any move whatsoever.

He had been her last hope. Two nights later, Francisco Madero and Pino Suárez were removed from the National Palace where they had been held, and transported by limousine—to the penitentiary, supposedly. But on a dark street just outside the walls of the prison, the two men were ordered from the cars by the men who had brought them there, and

Betrayals

shot in the head. The assassins then fired volleys of bullets into the automobiles, to make it look as though they had been attacked. The young drivers were warned that if they mentioned what they had seen, they too would be killed.

Again, one of the assassins was Cecilio Ocón, who had been first to strike a deathblow against Gustavo Madero at the *Ciudadela* a few days before. The second assassin was an army major who was immediately promoted to general by President Huerta. He would, in time, tell the whole story, and confess that he had acted under Huerta's explicit orders.

The official story, however, was that on the street that night, an attempt had been made to rescue Madero and Pino Suárez from the limousines, and that the two men had been shot in the ensuing gunfire. Henry Lane Wilson, taking the tragedy in stride, cabled his State Department, "I am disposed to accept the government's version of the affair."

Across the border, in Texas, Pancho Villa did not consider it a closed incident.

He had, on reaching Texas, written his former mentor Abraham González, once more serving as governor of Chihuahua: "I am at your services. I am the same Pancho Villa you knew in other days . . . Tell the President where I am; and tell him if he feels my presence would be harmful to Mexico, I will remain here in the United States, rather than cause his government any suffering. But if he ever needs me, I am ready to serve him, as I have always done . . .

"But to you, don Abraham, I beg you privately to let me take charge of some volunteers, because otherwise our cause is lost. Believe what I tell you . . ."

González had written back asking him to have patience, since his presence in Mexico at this time would indeed compromise Madero's government. However, he sent Villa money as a gift, in place of his army salary.

Then word reached Texas of the Huerta coup and Madero's imprisonment and death.

Villa knew that all too soon the same thing would happen in Chihuahua, and he turned immediately to the buying of guns and ammunition. It was while he was making these preparations that the kindly don Abraham—the first man of wealth and education who had ever treated Pancho Villa like an equal—was arrested in Chihuahua by Huerta's soldiers and put aboard a train bound for Mexico City and prison.

Like his chief, González never reached his destination. At lonely Bachimba Canyon, a couple of hours below the city of Chihuahua, the guards took him from the train, placed him under its wheels, and ran over him.

On March 28th, under cover of darkness, Pancho Villa crossed the river onto Mexican soil to avenge the deaths of the two men he had idolized, and to reopen the fight for their cause. His command consisted of eight men.

PART FOUR

Revolution Rekindled

CHAPTER 15

ONCE BACK IN their own land, Villa and his little band wasted no time. They bypassed the border town of Ciudad Juárez and moved rapidly south. A week after their arrival they were in the hills west of Chihuahua City, at the railway town of San Andrés where, two and a half years before, Villa had struck his first blow for the Revolution.

On the mayor's effusive assurances of support, the guerrilla leader moved on, picking up volunteers as he went—including, among others, his two brothers; and pausing after his first successful skirmish, at Santa Isabel, to announce his presence by telegram to the *Huertista* general Rábago.

"Señor General Antonio Rábago," the message read, "knowing that the government you represent is planning my extradition, I have come to save you the trouble. I am here in Mexico ready to fight the tyranny which you defend . . . [Signed] Pancho Villa."

Then he moved on, through the areas of Ciénega de Ortiz and Satevó where he had recruited so many men for the *Maderista* army before. Now they flocked to him again, from *haciendas*, and *ranchos*, and from villages, until his forces numbered nearly a thousand. Some of them came out of loyalty to Villa himself, some to fight for his cause. And some, as one of them told an American journalist, because "... it is good, fighting. You don't have to work in the mines . . ."

Near the *hacienda* of Chavarría, he had a windfall. He ambushed and seized a passenger train, and discovered aboard more than a hundred bars of silver, which had been shipped to Rábago for the purchase of military supplies. Villa and a small group of his men carried the silver to a lonely place in the mountains and buried it, for future use; then, doubled back north.

At Casas Grandes, site of the awesome pre-Spanish ruins and of Madero's first battle and defeat, he met his first substantial corps of government soldiers. In the fighting, *Huertista* losses were heavy in dead and wounded; and Villa took sixty prisoners. He lined them up three deep, to save ammunition, and had the whole group shot.

Since his outlaw days, he had been careless of human life—his own, as well as others'. When he had fought under army discipline, first for Madero and then in Huerta's army, he had perforce spared most of his prisoners. But now the deaths of Madero and Abraham González seemed to have unleashed a savagery in him; he no longer fought by the rules. From Casas Grandes on, he and his men would be absolutely ruthless.

Describing a U-shaped route from his point of entry into Mexico, Villa continued his way north toward Ascención, where he and his men set up camp. He had thought the place abandoned, but within a day or two, men began to straggle into town from the surrounding countryside. They turned out to be *Colorados*, left by the retreating forces of Pascual Orozco, who was back in Chihuahua again, collaborat-

Revolution Rekindled

ing with Huerta's army. As these men stayed to join Villa's army, women began to appear in camp too—*soldaderas*, wives and camp followers of the *Orozquistas*. Before long they were crouched over charcoal fires, cooking food for Villa's soldiers, bedding down with them, and stoically accepting the ways of war.

Subsequently, when Villa was reproved for treating these women with a lack of respect, he gave an indignant answer. "A woman is always a woman, and wherever there are men, they're going to get together. A woman acts of her own free will . . . Moreover, when we arrived here, there wasn't a woman around who hadn't already belonged to one or two *Orozquistas!*"

He was understandably annoyed. In the first place, such women had always been considered part of the spoils of a guerrilla war. And in the second—the reproof had been delivered to him by two emissaries from don Venustiano Carranza. Of all the men who espoused the Revolution, don Venustiano was the one he liked least. And it was don Venustiano who had set himself up as Villa's chief.

Venustiano Carranza, already fifty-four, was hardly the stereotype of a revolutionary. He was a trim, well-tailored man, given to combing his fingers nervously through his white beard; his weak eyes, light-sensitive, peered out at the world through blue-tinted glasses. He was one of fifteen children of a wealthy landowner of Coahuila; well-educated, he had twice been provisional governor of the state—once during Díaz's regime and once during Madero's. He had also been a supporter of Bernardo Reyes. In other words, he had at one time or another been on everybody's side.

But soon after Madero appeared upon the political scene, his opinions had begun to take shape—or so his public statements indicated. He complained that Madero had not gone far enough in his reforms. "The revolution which compromises," he said, "commits suicide!"

At the time of Huerta's overthrow of the Madero government, Carranza had been serving as elected governor of Coahuila. At first, he made a show of trying to reach a compromise with Huerta; but actually, he was using those first few days of national confusion to get his plans, and his small body of troops, ready for open revolt. It was typical of him that when he rebelled, he did so in a well-disciplined manner.

A few days after Madero's death, he took his stand. He sent off an angry wire to President Taft of the United States, denouncing Huerta as a usurper. He wired Ambassador Henry Lane Wilson in Mexico City, demanding Huerta's immediate resignation. He imposed forced loans on bankers and businessmen in his state, to finance his army; and at the end of February, marched his troops out of the state capital Saltillo. He hoped to establish a temporary capital at Piedras Negras, on the Texas border.

He was immediately involved in skirmishes with Huerta's troops. When he attempted to recapture Saltillo, he was roundly defeated. Retreating, he and his men took shelter at the *hacienda* Guadalupe, about halfway between Saltillo and Monclova, to the north. It was here, on the night of March 25th, 1913, that he conceived and dictated his "Plan of Guadalupe." This declaration demanded the resignation of Huerta and his government, and the establishment of a Constitutionalist army, with himself as its First Chief.

Whatever his other skills, however, he was not a first-rate general. A week after he had issued his plan, he met with delegates from the other large northern states, Sonora and Chihuahua, to discuss the appointment of a military chief for the newly created army.

The choice did not fall on Pancho Villa. Carranza was ambitious for power and jealous of anyone who threatened it; and he saw in the colorful Villa a potential rival. After

Revolution Rekindled

considering various other possible leaders, the delegates decided on a young rancher from Sonora, Alvaro Obregón.

Obregón, like Villa, had fought under Huerta against Pascual Orozco the preceding year; prior to that he had been raising chickpeas on the fertile soil of his native area of Huatabampo, near the coast of the Gulf of California. He was a widower, with two small children; good-natured, courageous in battle, not as cultured as Carranza but with an amazing memory and a practical, inventive intelligence.

There were those who disliked him as a "comedian"; and he had an unfortunate tendency toward flowery rhetoric in his speeches. But these were, perhaps, his only serious faults. As a soldier, he had already distinguished himself by his capture of Nogales, in northern Sonora, and much of the area below it. Now he was sweeping down through the coastal state of Sinaloa, to leave the *Huertista* forces isolated and under siege in the two seacoast towns of Guaymas and Mazatlán. He had infinite patience in battle, letting the enemy spend its strength against him, and then, when they were exhausted, striking and overwhelming them.

Carranza might well have seen in him a future rival, too, and rejected him as he had rejected Villa—but for one thing. Obregón had sent him a telegram, that spring of 1913, urging that no army chieftain be allowed to take public office, since, as he said, "all of our national misfortunes have been due to the unbridled ambitions of military men."

Here, then, was a man who would not threaten Carranza's future plans for himself. Alvaro Obregón was appointed chief of the Constitutionalist army; and Carranza sent two envoys off to Pancho Villa at Ascención, complaining about his army's "atrocities," and asking him to place himself under Obregón's command.

Hence Villa's irritation, during his interview with the two men at his headquarters at Ascención. He defended his troops' behavior; and, as for the appointment of this man Obregón as his military superior—ridiculous! Obregón knew as much about the terrain of Chihuahua as he, Pancho Villa, knew about Sonora!

The emissaries hastily agreed to give him all possible freedom of movement; and, grudgingly, Villa acquiesced. "Tell your don Venustiano Carranza," he said, "that I accept his Plan of Guadalupe, that I accept him as First Chief, and that I'm ready to obey him in all things concerning the Revolution and the people's interests. If he's really a revolutionary he can be sure of my friendship and my loyalty.

"But," he added, "when it comes to soldiering—tell him I won't accept anybody he sends to order me around. And if we're short of generals here, I'll appoint them myself!"

Villa's command was already strengthened, at this time, by the addition of Juan Medina, a former federal officer, in whose military judgment Villa placed great faith. As summer wore on he was joined by other chiefs and their men, among them Maclovio Herrera who had come up from Parral with four hundred men. Herrera had been a guerrilla leader; Villa grew fond of him, and called him, affectionately, "Big ears."

In late August, the combined troops attacked San Andrés —whose mayor, it seemed, remained a *Huertista* in spite of his protestations to Villa earlier in the year. It was an overwhelming victory for Villa. The town was strategically situated on the railroad; and several trainloads of supplies fell into his hands.

Morale was running high, now, among his troops; and he himself, in this and subsequent battles, increased his knowledge of military tactics. He learned to feint, to spread his opponents' defenses thin, and then to make a sudden attack where it was least expected.

By September he was moving south again, toward Jiménez, in southern Chihuahua, where he was joined by his old

Revolution Rekindled

friend Tomás Urbina and six hundred trained soldiers from Durango.

Urbina—boisterous as ever, and still more than half outlaw—had come fresh from capturing and sacking the city of Durango, and had brought with him more than half-a-million pesos in cash. He told Villa that Venustiano Carranza, knowing of his sudden riches, had asked him in the name of unity to contribute to the First Chief's cause. "I didn't refuse him," said Urbina. "I gave him sixty pesos and a broken-down saddle. Did I do right, *compadre?*"

Villa was laughing too hard to answer.

Urbina had also brought with him a soldier named Rodolfo Fierro, a former bandit and railroad worker, who would become the most reckless—and most-feared—man in Villa's army.

Early in autumn, Villa began to plan an attack on Torreón, in Coahuila. He had more than ten thousand men under his command by now and controlled most of the railroad line leading to the city. The Nazas River was in flood, but, he reasoned, it could be crossed by rafts. He, Villa, would take the intervening town of Avilés, with Tomás Urbina defending his flank; while Maclovio Herrera and his men would remain on the near side of the river to take Torreón's neighboring cities of Lerdo and Gómez Palacio.

They reached the Nazas—swollen now by the summer's rains—the end of September, when abruptly, Villa stopped. It had occurred to him that while his fellow officers were responsible for the lives of several thousands of their own men, the order of command had never really been approved by them. On the advice of Juan Medina, a council of all commanders was held. The *División del Norte*, the Northern Division, was created out of this meeting; and Pancho Villa was chosen as its commander.

The two branches of the army attacked, and defeated,

Federalist forces in the towns neighboring Torreón; and with the help of a competent artillery (much of it captured at Avilés), Villa began to pound the federals' forward positions on the hillsides immediately outside the city. After more than twenty-four hours of heavy fighting, Torreón was in the hands of the *División del Norte*.

Villa entered the city at ten o'clock that night, to the cheers of the occupants and the sound of band music. He had, however, left instructions with Rodolfo Fierro that the captured enemy officers, in accordance with Venustiano Carranza's recent orders, were to be shot. Fierro and two fellow officers chose some eighty victims, and had made a game of shooting them down with their pistols.

Within the city, celebrations for Villa's victory went on much of the night; and before dawn, the victorious general was wakened by an orchestra on the sidewalk under his hotel window, playing the lovely "Las Mañanitas"—a song sung just before dawn, to children throughout Mexico on their birthday or saint's day. After the night's wild celebration, and the bloody reprisals at the army's encampment outside town, the gentle melody was remarkably inappropriate.

Villa, who had merely been following Carranza's instructions in ordering the executions, and was unaware of the method used, felt no pangs of conscience. He busied himself distributing to the poor the food and clothing his men had captured. He dug into his army's surgical supplies, to alleviate a crying need in the local hospitals. Some of his generosity was paid for by forced loans he extracted from the city's banks.

The capture of Torreón was a welcome victory. It had cut lines of communication between federal troops in the north and those in central Mexico; and the retreating forces had abandoned guns, ammunition, and pieces of heavy artillery which Villa knew would be invaluable. But it was only one of many cities he must capture before the northern states were free of *Federalistas*. Ciudad Juárez, for instance—the gateway between Mexico and the United States—must be taken. And the city of Chihuahua.

Chihuahua City would be difficult; most of the soldiers stationed there were Orozco's *Colorados*, as skilled in guerrilla fighting and hand-to-hand combat as Villa's own men. But the enemy was off balance now, and Villa knew he must strike quickly.

CHAPTER 16

ON NOVEMBER 5th, 1913, the Villa forces struck Chihuahua City; and for three days and nights the battle went on. But Villa did not have ammunition or supplies enough to continue the fight at such a pace, and the third night, withdrew a short way to the south. When the enemy tried to give chase, the *Villistas* retaliated with such force that the *Colorados* pulled back to the security of the city and stayed there, expecting a lengthy siege.

Villa, however, left in position only enough of his men to maintain the impression of a siege. The others he moved in a forced all-night march to the north, bypassing the city under cover of darkness, and reaching El Sauz, on the north-central railroad line, before anyone knew he was not still poised on the southern outskirts of Chihuahua.

Here, thanks to information he had received from one of his spies in Ciudad Juárez, he ambushed a coal train heading south toward Chihuahua from the border town. He also took prisoner the engineer and the telegrapher.

He then divided his troops again, sending twenty-five hundred of them north. However, if they failed to reach Ciudad

Revolution Rekindled

Juárez, he said, it didn't matter; the two thousand he kept with him would be enough for his purposes.

He left the *Huertista* engineer under guard at the controls of the train, and placed one of his own telegraphers with a pistol at the shoulder of the captive telegrapher. "Send this message to Ciudad Juárez," he ordered the captive. "'Derailed here. Revolutionaries have destroyed telegraph wires and train tracks south to Chihuahua. Send instructions and another locomotive to get me back on the tracks.'"

The message was tapped out. Ciudad Juárez answered that there was no locomotive to spare; the engineer must find tools and solve his own problem. Then he must wire for further instructions.

Villa waited for two hours, till the coal was removed from the train and his two thousand men entrained in its place; then ordered the telegrapher to send another wire. "On tracks. No rail or telegraph south. Big cloud of dust visible, may be Revolutionaries. I need instructions."

The instructions in answer read: "Start back here. Ask for orders at each station."

The train started up—northbound, this time. At each station, the captive telegrapher tapped out a request for further orders, and received each time the code letter for "Continue."

The locomotive continued north. Just before midnight, it drew near Ciudad Juárez. It went on, unmolested, past the city's defense lines, and on into the station. Here, with a *Villista* pistol at his head, the engineer brought the train to a stop.

Because the train's arrival had been announced long since, it created no stir. What was not expected, however, were the two thousand Villa soldiers who poured out of the boxcars, flooding across the railroad yard and fanning out into every street in the city.

Within two hours, Ciudad Juárez belonged to the *División del Norte;* the Federalist officers had taken refuge in the city jail; and Juan Medina, Villa's chief of staff, was gathering up three thousand pesos from the tables of the gambling houses, while the astonished gamblers, both Mexican and North American, looked on.

The Federalist general, however, had been allowed to escape, on Villa's orders. He was Francisco Castro, who had tried to intervene last year when Villa had been looking down the rifle barrels of Huerta's firing squad. Villa was ruthless with his enemies, but he rarely forgot an act of kindness.

He also rewarded young "Carlitos"—the clerk Carlos Jáuregui who had helped him escape prison in Mexico City. He gave him control of the keno games in Ciudad Juárez. The poker and crap games and the roulette monopolies he gave to his brother Hipólito.

Ciudad Juárez had fallen November 15th, 1913. Five days later, Villa learned that Huerta forces were coming north in strength from Chihuahua City, to counterattack. Already they were nearing Samalayuca, on the railroad lines to the south; and he badly needed one day for preparation.

He sent the daredevil Rodolfo Fierro down to intercept them at Samalayuca, to damage their trains and delay them any way he could. Then, leaving only fifty men in charge of Ciudad Juárez, he made a vast show of reviewing his troops— to reassure the people of the city—and marched them a short distance southwest, to the dry plains known as Tierra Blanca.

Here he distributed his men along a front more than five miles wide; weak, perhaps, at some points, but with reserves ready to move in rapidly wherever needed. He knew this would be, in all likelihood, the definitive battle of the Revolution; and that if he lost Ciudad Juárez, with its access to arms and ammunition from the United States, the Revolutionaries

Revolution Rekindled

could lose all of Chihuahua—if not all of Mexico. What he needed now was a monumental victory.

The federal troop trains moved into sight; and then, for reasons unknown to Villa, paused. They remained there in the distance overnight. But at dawn the next morning, the 23rd, the fighting began.

Villa had so chosen the field of battle that the *Huertista* troops would have no access to water or supplies; while he, Villa, had the train from Juárez at his back, to keep him supplied with everything he needed. And so it proved: food, water, and ammunition arrived regularly; and the wounded were quickly transported back to the city. Blankets and medical equipment came from sympathizers in El Paso, and money from as far away as New York. In Ciudad Juárez, well-to-do families, both Mexican and American, converted their homes into hospitals.

Villa fought brilliantly. Every time one portion of his line was threatened, he attacked the enemy from another, relieving the pressure on the weaker points. The enemy's artillery bogged down in the sand and could not move. One of the *Huertista* flanks broke and fled in retreat; only the screen of dust kept the men from being ridden down and destroyed.

By evening of November 25th, what was left of the federal force was in full retreat. One section fled by train. But Rodolfo Fierro gave chase on horseback, amid a hail of bullets; leaped from his horse to the platform; ran along the roofs of the cars until he reached the brake cylinder, opened it, and stopped the train. At that point Fierro's scouts and Villa's own *dorados* threw themselves on the cars, and the battle of Tierra Blanca ended in a holocaust for the federal troops.

Villa knew the defeated Federalists had not gone back to Chihuahua, but had fled eastward, toward Ojinaga; and that there was now a general exodus from Chihuahua City of the rich, the Huerta sympathizers, and even of the two hundred Federalist troops left there to guard the city. So, on the third of December, he started south with his troops to complete the conquest.

It was while his army was moving south toward the capital that the last of the dynastic rulers of Chihuahua—the Terrazas family—decided that their way of life was ended. Old don Luis Terrazas had tried to stave off the inevitable by paying Pascual Orozco to fight the Revolutionaries; but now even Orozco had fled to Ojinaga.

So, leaving only young don Luis behind to dispose of the family holdings, the Terrazas clan had put a few belongings into their chauffeur-driven car; and, along with five thousand Orozco soldiers and sympathizers, set out to cross the hundred miles of dusty, bitter cold Chihuahua desert that lay between the capital city and Ojinaga, on the Rio Grande to the east.

On the fifth of December, Chihuahua City delivered itself to Pancho Villa without resistance; and Villa, to give the state at least nominal government, declared himself governor.

"Governor of Chihuahua." It was a far cry from being a peon on the *rancho* Gogojito. Or an outlaw, hounded by the *rurales* through the Durango hills!

There remained, however, all those federal forces now in Ojinaga, who during December had badly defeated the two detachments Villa had sent against them. Villa acceded to Carranza's request that Manuel Chao take over the governorship; and, the night of January 6th, 1914, started a forced march eastward, with two brigades.

It was a grueling trip. Over a hundred miles of wintry desert lay between Chihuahua and Ojinaga. Traveling light in order to travel fast, Villa's men "liberated" cattle from the *ranchos* along the way, and roasted or ate raw the freshly butchered meat. They slept little, and in three days they were within sight of the low mesa where the town was situated.

To one side were the yellowish waters of the Rio Grande, with the tiny town of Presidio visible on the American side. Almost every house in Ojinaga was damaged; it had been taken and lost five times. Now Villa scanned the surrounding terrain, and figured it would be an easy fight—if his men were in the right frame of mind.

He made a great show of being casual: stretched out lazily on the ground and, chewing a straw, he told his men it shouldn't take them more than an hour and a half to capture the enemy garrison the next day.

The detachments which had preceded them there earlier in the winter, and had already suffered serious losses to the *Federales,* took heart. That night, as everyone prepared for tomorrow's fight, Villa heard them singing.

They attacked in the morning. In sixty-five minutes the city had fallen; Pascual Orozco and the federal commander—and countless numbers of their men—were fleeing across the Rio Grande. Villa had swept the state of Chihuahua clean.

CHAPTER 17

ON HIS RETURN to Chihuahua City, Villa circumvented the rule of Carranza's puppet governor Manuel Chao by establishing his own military government. He set his soldiers to work as policemen, bakers, streetcar conductors, butchers—even street sweepers. He ordered the execution of any soldier found drunk. And, within a single month, he started construction on forty schools.

He expropriated the lands of the Terrazas and others, dividing it up into sixty-acre farms, and giving it to disabled veterans of the Revolution, or to the survivors of men killed in action. The *hacienda* cattle he sent to the border for sale to the United States or ordered butchered for sale to the poor at a fraction of its worth. His sweep through Mexico, later, would be marked by the sight of his horsemen, in their boots and spurs, cartridge belts and huge sombreros, presiding over the distribution of confiscated beef, the freshly butchered cuts spread out at street crossings, as excited children carried home more meat than they had seen in a lifetime.

And he began printing money. Carranza, who had begun the business of issuing unsecured paper currency, was not sending him enough—a problem Villa solved by printing his own. These paper bills became known as *bilimbiques*—perhaps, as one historian suggests, because in pre-Revolutionary days, a mining foreman named William Viques had paid his workers with signed vouchers instead of cash; and his name came to be synonymous with paper vouchers of dubious value.

A number of lawyers and businessmen sympathetic to the rebel cause advised Villa, as tactfully as possible, that it was not good economic policy to issue paper money without gold or silver behind it, but Villa ignored them.

However, the *bilimbiques* only solved part of the problem. An army *and* a military government were proving an expensive combination. How to raise more money?

Villa discovered that the younger don Luis Terrazas was still in Chihuahua. Convinced that much of the Terrazas wealth had been converted into gold and hidden, he turned the hapless Terrazas junior over to his aide, Rodolfo Fierro. Fierro used his own methods to elicit a confession from the former *hacendado*; and in short order Villa and a couple of his men were in the Banco Minero de Chihuahua, drilling into one of the pillars of the lobby. It contained more than six hundred thousand pesos in gold coins.

Typically, Villa made it immediately available to his officers. "Take what you need," he said.

He had not intended to keep any of the money for his personal use; but there were still forty thousand pesos he had left in a cabinet in his house, while he decided what to do with it. One day he found the money gone; and soon discovered that it had been stolen by the mother and sister of his current "wife," Juana Torres.

Juana was one of several girls he had found it expedient to "marry," at one time or another. He was still legally married to Luz Corral, but had developed a comforting philosophy about his other women. A "marriage ceremony" made the girls happy, he had discovered, and certainly no official was going to prosecute him, Pancho Villa, for bigamy. As for the priest—"Just threaten to put a bullet through his head," he suggested to one of his young staff members. "You'll see how fast he comes round!"

Hence, it was as his "mother-in-law" and "sister-in-law" that the two other women of his household went to jail, over Juana's tears and protestations. And in a short time, a letter she had smuggled to them fell into his hands.

It deplored Villa's cruelty to them. "But what can I do with this bandit?" she had written. "My life with him is a torment . . . He is a bad man, bloodthirsty and without heart . . . His behavior toward me is worse than death."

For a moment, reading her words, Villa wanted to kill her. Juana, for whom he had done so many kindnesses! Then, controlling himself, he went to her room. "Juana," he said, "read me this letter. You know how badly I read . . ."

Juana paled when she saw the letter. At last, at his insistence, she read it aloud. Watching her terror, he was overwhelmed by a momentary pity for her. But the words of the letter were so insulting that he steeled himself.

"Maybe I'm just an ignoramus who doesn't understand things very well," he said. "Read it again. Let me hear what it says about me."

Weeping, trembling in panic, she read it again.

Well, he had loved her. But he didn't any longer. He left her, freed her mother and sister from prison, and just in case the women *were* innocent, gave them enough money to leave Chihuahua.

The next person who aroused his fury was not so lucky.

Until now, Villa had been a popular figure in the American imagination. The newspapers portrayed him as a sort of Robin Hood, robbing the rich to give to the poor. In spite of an official arms embargo, guns and ammunition had poured over the border from sympathizers across the Rio Grande. With one reckless act, however, he changed from folk-hero to villain overnight.

William Benton, an irascible Scot with large holdings in Chihuahua, came to Villa's headquarters one cold day in February, 1914, in a rage at Villa's expropriation of some of his land and cattle. In the ensuing argument he made a move toward his pistol, and Villa promptly had him arrested. On the advice of Rodolfo Fierro, he sentenced him to be shot. Fierro took him, handcuffed, to Samalayuca; had a grave dug for him in the sandy soil; killed him with a blow on the back of the head, and buried him on the spot, handcuffs and all.

There were outraged protests from the United States, acting on England's behalf. They demanded that Benton's body be restored to his widow. Villa, who had informed them that Benton had been executed by a firing squad for threatening his life, was in a quandary. If he exhumed Benton's body and delivered it to the American authorities, they would discover that Benton had not been shot. Fierro, whose fault it was, dug up the body and shot it, but was advised by the brigade's doctor that this ruse would be easily detected.

Villa was forced to appeal to Carranza for advice. The Constitutionalist chief ordered him to issue no more statements, but to maintain utter silence. In due time, he advised, the scandal would die down.

As, during the greater violence yet to come, it did.

But it was not forgotten; and there would be a time when the "Benton affair" would be an important factor in Villa's political life—and that of Mexico as well.

Villa's army was not the only one to be guilty of atrocities. They occurred generally, all over the country—but nowhere on such a grand scale as in Mexico City, where President Victoriano Huerta, since his accession to office the preceding spring, had been busy wiping out every evidence of disaffection. Within ten days of his assuming the presidency, his troops had been called out to Santa Julia, on the outskirts of Mexico City, where they machine-gunned a crowd of protesters, killing more than a hundred.

Huerta continued to have the fervent support of the United States ambassador, Henry Lane Wilson, however; and perhaps this made him reckless. Time and again, *Huertista* generals forced their way into the military prison or the penitentiary, and dragged former *Maderista* sympathizers—sometimes forty at a time—out to be shot "while attempting to escape."

Huerta made no effort to stop the bloodshed. He himself spent so much time drunk that it was not uncommon to see, at various hours of the day or night, limousines cruising the streets of downtown Mexico City, taking his staff members from one saloon to another, to look for their chief executive.

No matter. Henry Lane Wilson's fear of the common people of Mexico was so great that he tolerated any and all of Huerta's foibles. He kept up a barrage of wires and letters to his State Department, declaring that Huerta's presidency was hailed by Mexicans everywhere, and urged prompt recognition of the regime. He ignored information from his consuls in the north of Mexico that the states of Sonora, Chihuahua, and Coahuila were in open revolt; and not once but several times notified his government that the respected Venustiano Carranza had surrendered unconditionally to the *Huertistas*—a complete fiction.

Fortunately, the United States did not rely for its information on the ambassador's dispatches alone; eyewitness accounts and dispatches of consular officials told an altogether different story; and on July 17, 1913, Ambassador Wilson had sailed for home, recalled by the recently inaugurated President Woodrow Wilson (to whom he was not related).

Huerta's excesses continued unchecked. In September, a

senator from the state of Chiapas, Dr. Belisario Domínguez, proposed to deliver a speech to the Senate denouncing the failures and cruelty of the Huerta regime, referring to Huerta as a "bloody and ferocious soldier, who does not hesitate to kill when obstructed." The statement urged members of the Senate to "cast out the shame of having as first magistrate a traitor and assassin."

The Senate refused to allow Domínguez to deliver the speech, but copies of it reached the individual senators and deputies, and within two weeks the senator was arrested at his hotel, taken to the cemetery of the tree-shaded, ancient colonial suburb of Coyoacán, and shot. His body was left lying in a ditch.

The Senate, intimidated, made no protest, but the Chamber of Deputies was infuriated. When they raised a public outcry, Huerta threw two hundred and ten of them into prison. The Senate he merely dissolved.

On the orders of his government, the American chargé d'affaires sent word of Woodrow Wilson's shock at the "lawless methods employed by General Huerta"; and, a few days later, President Wilson himself made a public reference to Huerta's rule as "usurpation." "If General Huerta does not retire," he said, ". . . it will become the duty of the United States to use less peaceful means to put him out."

A former professor and college president, Woodrow Wilson was a profound believer in the democratic process. Certainly his aims were more idealistic than those of William Howard Taft. He wanted to put an end to the "dollar diplomacy" of his predecessor, and support only those countries which had truly representative governments. No matter how admirable his motives, however, he tended to overlook the desire of his near neighbors to make their own political choices. Historically, it was a common American failing. "I propose," he said apropos of Mexico that autumn of 1913, "to teach the South American republics to elect good men!"

He thoroughly disapproved of Huerta. He thought Villa was "not as bad as he had been painted"; and considered Carranza the best of the three. His doubts about Villa's fitness for political leadership were deepened, the following February, by the killing of William Benton.

In the early spring of 1914, Villa did not think of himself as a political leader—at least, not consciously. He deeply disliked Carranza, but for the sake of unity among the Revolutionary forces, continued to support him.

In fact, Carranza's dogmatism, and his need to be surrounded by sycophants who would agree with everything he said, alienated not a few Revolutionaries. Villa discovered that the magnificent artillery commander, former Federalist Felipe Angeles, was unhappy serving under the First Chief, and wrote Carranza asking that Angeles be transferred to his command.

Felipe Angeles was a tall, slender, thoughtful, almost saintly man, the opposite of Villa in every way. But he had great admiration for Villa's military skill, and respected his honest devotion to the Revolutionary cause. Villa, on his part, had equal respect for Angeles. He remembered that Angeles had been jailed with Madero, and only by good luck had not been killed at his leader's side. He celebrated Angeles's arrival in Chihuahua with parades, and banquets, and sought him out as a dinner companion thereafter, asking his advice not only on military matters, but even, humbly, about table manners.

It was well that Angeles had joined Villa; the *División del Norte* needed a strong artillery for the campaign Villa was planning. Huerta's Federalists had retaken Torreón and the towns surrounding it, and were now concentrating their forces in the Laguna district, the rich cotton-growing area at the juncture of northeastern Durango and the southwest tip of Coahuila. They must be driven out.

Much of this area Villa was already familiar with: two years before, he had fought his way across it under Huerta; and his own successful battle for Torreón had taken place less than six months ago. He made careful preparation. He wrote the commander of the Northeastern Division, Pablo González, to make a diversionary attack on Monterrey and Saltillo, to the east. He assembled the artillery pieces recently captured from the Federalists; and flatcars for their transportation. He had well-equipped hospital cars; boxcars for horses, cattle, and troops; and cabooses, like the one he had often traveled in, for his officers. Many of his regular soldiers would ride on top of the cars, as usual. There were automobiles; and he had investigated, and discarded, the idea of an airplane.

They set out from Chihuahua the middle of March, reaching the Sierra de Conejos in the midst of an early storm. He left most of his trains at Escalón; and, in a quick, many-pronged attack, took the enemy outposts of Personál, Tlahualilo, and Bermejillo in a single day. It was from Bermejillo that Felipe Angeles telephoned the Federalist general in command of the Laguna district and asked him to save the lives of many of their countrymen by surrendering Torreón.

The Federalist general was startled to find the *Villistas* already in Bermejillo, but refused the invitation to surrender. Soon after, he phoned back. This time he got Villa on the line, and told him that he and his men were "coming to get him" in a few minutes.

"Come ahead," said Villa cordially. "We'll be glad to welcome you."

"Then get supper ready."

"There are plenty of people here to feed you."

"Well—as I said, we're on our way."

"Fine, señor. But if you don't want to bother, we'll come out and meet you. We've traveled a long way, just for the pleasure of seeing you. And my men and I are tired chasing around the country looking for you."

"Are there many of you?"

"Not so many, señor. Just a couple of artillery regiments and about ten thousand fellows I brought along to entertain you."

His next attack, two days later, was on the enemy's new line, closer to Torreón. Villa and his own brigade attacked Gómez Palacio, on the near side of the Nazas River, and suffered heavy losses, as did the other sections of his army. However, within the next few days, the Revolutionaries had taken nearby Lerdo and, circling, had severed the federals' railroad line to the east, to cut off their supplies and reinforcements from the industrial city of Monterrey—which Carranza's General Pablo González had failed to attack.

Villa now concentrated much of his strength on the battle for Gómez Palacio, only a few miles from his target city. The battle went on for seventy-two hours without respite. The enemy artillery pounded Felipe Angeles's emplacements, and he responded in kind; casualties were heavy. Advances made at night were lost in the morning. But at last, the end of the third day, Villa realized that a silence had fallen. He suspected the enemy had withdrawn.

As he and his men moved cautiously into the city, they saw mute evidence of the three-day battle: the shattered houses, streets littered with the bodies of men and horses—but no sign of the Federalist troops.

The next night, as Villa relaxed after a day of restoring order, he could see flames at the top of La Pila, the hill which had protected the city from his advance, and for which he and Angeles had fought so bitterly. Now, at its summit, his men were burning the dead of both sides, and the fire licked red against the night sky.

He fell into one of his rare moments of contemplation. "Those men were fighting up there day-before-yesterday," he thought. ". . . Men who wanted to take that hill, and men who didn't want them to take it. Now they're being burned,

Revolution Rekindled

and they don't even know who won or who lost. Señor, what a profound thing war is! How many men like those have to die, so others can live and flourish! How many dead it costs, for the cause of the people to go forward!"

The way cleared now, he began his bombardment of emplacements in Torreón March 28th. Other Revolutionary units were attacking hills surrounding the city. Fighting was relentless; but by the first of April, a few of the Revolutionary forces had penetrated the city, and were fighting hand-to-hand.

The next day, the enemy guns fell silent, as they had done at Gómez Palacio. Villa had, before the battle, ordered that one route be left open for a Federalist retreat—and the Federalists had taken it.

There had been, in all, eleven days of ceaseless fighting. The *División del Norte*'s losses came to more than five hundred dead, fifteen hundred wounded; the enemy losses were still greater.

Villa had promised himself to take Torreón, with his teeth if necessary. He had almost had to do just that.

CHAPTER 18

ONLY TEN DAYS LATER, Villa and his men were attacking the Federalists at San Pedro de las Colonias, some fifty miles to the east. This time his enemy included not only the *Huertista* forces who had retreated from Torreón but fresh troops from Saltillo and elsewhere. Villa's men were still worn out from the long battle for Torreón and the smaller fights and skirmishes they had engaged in immediately after, on the way to San Pedro. Even their horses were suffering; some had worn saddles so long their saddle blankets were stuck to their skin.

But Villa knew that if the *Huertistas* had a chance to prepare their defenses, it could be fatal; hence the speed and relentlessness of his attack. The battle, which began at three-thirty in the morning, was over before noon, and Villa wired Carranza a list of more than twenty Federalist generals who had been defeated in the action.

Carranza, by now, was in Chihuahua City; and his responses to Villa's written and telegraphed requests had been cool. When Villa asked for permission to execute a couple of his officers who had refused to obey orders under fire, Carranza took them under his own wing. Then there was the matter of Pablo González, commander of the Northeastern Division—Carranza's personal appointee, in spite of the fact that he had never won a battle. Prior to the attack on Torreón, Villa had wired González to cut the Federalists' railroad line from the east, and González had not done so. But Villa's complaint about this to Carranza fell on deaf ears.

As did Villa's complaints about Manuel Chao, Carranza's puppet governor of Chihuahua. Chao and Villa were constantly at cross-purposes over the governing of the state, and Villa wanted him removed.

In fact, though Villa had repeated many times to the First Chief that he had no political ambitions, and no desires for himself other than to serve Carranza in the best interests of Mexico, Carranza seemed to do everything he could to check Villa's growing popularity and to encourage his enemies.

So Villa returned to Chihuahua City for a talk with his chief, to straighten some of these matters out. He went to the interview prepared to show the older man the respect and honor he felt was due him—but as he gave Carranza his first emotional *abrazo*, Carranza's coldness chilled his blood. And as they spoke, the First Chief would not even look him in the eye.

"I realized," said Villa later, "that I could not open my heart to him, because for him I was not a friend but a rival . . . I believed then that this man was not the interpreter of the hopes of the peasants, but a clerk—the owner of an *hacienda*." And then, the final judgment, "He wanted, at whatever cost, the presidency of Mexico, and I wanted many things for my country which he could not even understand."

Villa kept his feelings to himself, however; and in mid-April, something happened between the United States and Mexico which dwarfed all else.

Since February, the United States' embargo on the shipment of war materials to Mexico had been lifted, and arms and ammunition had been flowing freely to the rebels of Sonora, Chihuahua, and Coahuila. This was a bitter brew for Victoriano Huerta, who was struggling to keep his hold on a country which did not want him. Just as Woodrow Wilson, in Washington, was looking for a pretext to intervene on behalf of the Constitutionalists, Huerta was growing increasingly ready to challenge his gigantic neighbor.

Even in his cups, as he was most of the time, Huerta was canny. He knew how sensitive his fellow Mexicans were to foreign interference because of the Mexican-American war of 1846–48. He knew that any overt threat to Mexico's sovereignty would bring all his countrymen, of whatever political belief, into one armed camp; that Federalist and Revolutionary would forget their differences in the face of a common enemy.

Or did he? Surely he could not have been so drunk, either with alcohol or his own power, that he would all but provoke American intervention. Yet that was what he did.

But a still greater share of the blame, and shame, must fall upon the well-meant but inexcusable high-handedness of the Woodrow Wilson government, that spring of 1914.

The incident took place at the busy tropical port of Tampico, on the Gulf of Mexico. So many of the region's oil wells and refineries were owned by American interests, that Mexicans referred to it as *gringolandia*; and it was only to be expected, now the Federalist port was under siege by the Revolutionaries, that ships of the American navy would be

Revolution Rekindled 125

hovering offshore, to make sure no harm befell American property.

On the evening of April 9th, local Federalist officials discovered that an American tanker—no doubt unwittingly—was loading up in a restricted zone, in violation of siege restrictions. They arrested eight of the American crew members and took them off to jail.

The prisoners were quickly released, with a note of apology from the local Federalist commander; but the incident had already given the United States the justification it needed. Admiral Henry T. Mayo refused to accept the apology, but demanded a twenty-one-gun salute to the American flag.

Huerta refused, unless the American admiral would salute his flag in exchange—an act which would, in effect, amount to United States' recognition of the Huerta regime. Admiral Mayo refused.

While this solemn ballet of national honor was taking place, the Americans discovered that a German steamer, filled to the gunwales with machine guns and cartridges for the Huerta army, was due to arrive next day at Veracruz, four hundred miles down the coast.

The arms and ammunition would strengthen Huerta's forces immeasurably—just what the Americans did not want. There were hurried midnight conferences in Washington. The Americans could not stop the shipment at sea—after all, it was a German ship in international waters—but if they got control of the harbor at Veracruz, they could prevent the ship's landing. Woodrow Wilson's Secretary of the Navy sent a peremptory cable to Admiral Mayo, saying "Take Veracruz at once"; and on the morning of April 21st, troops from the United States Atlantic Fleet went ashore. They were met by armed *Veracruzanos* and by Mexico's naval cadets.

By evening, the calm and lovely peak of Orizaba looked

down over streets littered with more than three hundred Mexican dead. A score of Americans also lost their lives. The only beneficiaries in the whole tragic action were the vultures, which had taken flight at the first burst of gunfire, and were now circling back and flapping hideously down to investigate their prey.

Mexican response was immediate and almost unanimous. Huerta threatened to invade Texas in reprisal, arm Southern Negroes, and march on Washington. His opponent Venustiano Carranza issued an equally furious denunciation of the U.S. action, though he insisted that Huerta did not represent the Mexican people and had no right to speak for them.
Obregón's statement was in much the same vein.
Pancho Villa was the only leader, in fact, who did not let nationalism blind him to one serious fact: that in the case of a real war between Mexico and the United States, the Revolutionary forces would have to combine with Huerta's, and that would mean the end of the Revolution. He went quickly to Ciudad Juárez and got in touch with an American official he knew, to find out if United States really intended to make war on Mexico.
On being assured to the contrary, he said, "All right, señor. Tell President Wilson there won't be war between him and the Constitutionalists if he doesn't declare war on Mexico. And in wanting to hurt Huerta, he should commit no more acts of hostility." The following day he summoned newspapermen, and made a formal statement. ". . . The American people helped us with their friendship in our fight in 1910, as they are helping us now. If Victoriano Huerta looks for war, neither the United States nor we will let ourselves be fooled, even in spite of señor Carranza's reply to President Wilson . . . President Carranza, in his good intention, defends the honor of our country, but he does not mean

Revolution Rekindled

to declare war on the United States, nor do any of our Revolutionaries."

Carranza's reaction to Villa's news conference was surprisingly mild. He merely asked Villa to make no more such statements in the future.

However, on a visit to Villa's headquarters in Torreón soon after, he made a speech which was like a cold bath to the fiery spirits of Villa's soldiers. His Constitutionalist program, he said, was not a revolutionary one; nor was he himself a Revolutionary.

And when Villa told him he wanted to move south and take Zacatecas, the First Chief forbade it. Villa must continue east, he said, further into Coahuila, and capture the state capital Saltillo.

Villa was dismayed. He knew that Saltillo was manned by exhausted and ill-supplied Federalist troops, so that even an inept general like Pablo González could take it without difficulty. He could also guess why Carranza did not want him to move farther south: Zacatecas was in a direct line along the central plateau toward Mexico City, and the ambitious Carranza did not want Villa's powerful army any closer to the nation's capital than his own.

Once again, Villa obeyed, but the doubts, resentments, and dislike between the two men were increasing; it was only a matter of time before their real feelings erupted.

By mid-May, Villa's army had overcome the heaviest concentration of *Huertista* forces, at Paredón, on the rail line to the east. They moved on to the now vulnerable Saltillo, which the Federalists abandoned without a struggle. There, Villa established order, exacted forced loans for the care of the poor, and delivered the city to Pablo González—who had, in the meantime, finally won a battle: the rich oil center of Tampico.

González seemed, to Villa, a man of good will—not aggressive enough, perhaps, to be a good general, but disposed to be Villa's friend. As they strolled about the central plaza of Saltillo one May evening, Villa told him that when he took Zacatecas, he would pause there until González's forces, and Obregón's and his own, could meet and move on together in one grand triumphal procession to Mexico City.

But alas for Mexico, that was not the way it happened.

Since the suspension of hostilities at Veracruz, American and Mexican diplomats were meeting in Canada, trying to work out their mutual problems and to agree on a provisional government for Mexico which would be acceptable to everyone. But while those talks progressed, the unity of the Constitutionalists, in northern Mexico, was breaking apart.

Carranza had recently issued a press statement depreciating Francisco Madero and his supporters and referring to Villa as a "bandit." Now, in a further effort to divide and rule, he appointed a chief for the Zacatecas assault—not Villa, who had been chafing for the assignment, but Panfilo Natera, who, along with the Arrieta brothers, was a known enemy of Villa. Natera was the *Villista* general who had been so badly beaten the previous winter at Ojinaga before Villa's arrival there.

Villa was furious. But he contained his fury, and waited, knowing that Carranza's hand-picked generals could not possibly take Zacatecas.

Sure enough, in a short time he received a wire from the First Chief, ordering him to send troops and artillery to the hard-pressed General Natera.

Villa wired back his readiness to go as soon as the railroad lines to the south were repaired, a matter of only a few days. But Carranza did not want Villa. He wanted Villa's troops and artillery *without* Villa.

Villa had created the *División del Norte*, and it was clear that he and he alone knew how to dispose its units to make it the most powerful striking force in the country. But its separate divisions, without himself in command, could be massacred. Accordingly, then, he played his strongest card: he resigned his commission, and asked whom he should appoint in his place.

Carranza in a terse telegram of response accepted the resignation. As for a successor to Villa, he wired, the generals could choose their own.

By now, however, Villa's generals had all read the series of telegrams, and sent their own wires, insisting on their intention to proceed to Zacatecas as ordered—with Villa at their head.

Carranza repeated that their commander could be anyone but Villa. But the generals replied that Villa was indispensable to the success of the army and the Revolution, and that they were marching south under his command.

Even General Chao, whom Villa had only recently threatened with arrest, sent his own wire of support for Villa. And as for hotheaded Maclovio Herrera, of the big ears—he pulled his pistol at the telegrapher, and ordered him to send a wire saying,

DON VENUSTIANO CARRANZA, SALTILLO. YOU ARE A SONOFABITCH. [SIGNED] MACLOVIO HERRERA.

Within two days, the first trainloads of *Villista* troops began to roll out of the station at Torreón, bound for Zacatecas.

CHAPTER 19

THE FIRST DETACHMENT of *Villista* troops to move south were under the command of Villa's old friend from outlaw days, Tomás Urbina, the "Lion of Durango." The artillery followed the day after, under the quiet, dignified Felipe Angeles; he and Urbina would take up positions east and south of the hilltops protecting Zacatecas, and lay out a tentative plan of operations, pending Villa's arrival. The generals Carranza had sent down earlier had withdrawn to safety after their defeats and would cooperate with Villa's plans.

Villa, in Torreón, took time off to get cash for his venture. He seized a whole printing of Carranza's paper money, and the money-printing dies as well. He wired Alvaro Obregón —now in Tepic and well along in his sweep along the coast and the western sierra—asking for further support; but Obregón's answer was a tactful refusal. Villa was on his own.

On the twenty-second of June, his train pulled in at a small town above Zacatecas. He checked over his generals' plan of battle, and inspected the placement of their batteries. He was shown the directions from which Natera, Chao, Herrera, Raul Madero, and other leaders would approach, and the

Revolution Rekindled

treacherous ravines which would make a Federalist retreat to the south almost impossible.

All told, his own army numbered twenty-three thousand men. The enemy, he knew, had about twelve thousand, but strong artillery and a great deal more ammunition.

He looked forward to the morrow with a feeling of excitement. It would be a great battle, he thought.

Seventy-five hundred feet above sea level, its houses clinging to hillsides and its cobbled roads plunging down into ravines, the quaint old town of Zacatecas had provided a wealth in silver to the Spaniards through the whole colonial period. The area was still a honeycomb of ancient mine shafts. The air above was thin and cold; wind whistled through the passes, and the rain—which was falling bitter cold this dark June night—drained quickly off the streets and down into the ravines, to disappear into the ever thirsty ground. Like other rains, it would flood the old mines, but leave behind, as always, no drinking water for the Zacatecans.

It was especially cruel to the *Villista* soldiers, who had no capes to protect themselves with as they went about their work. Under cover of the dark and wet, they were busy moving cannon and machine guns from their previous emplacements, which for several days had been visible to the Federalist soldiers, to other situations, better hidden. Next morning the Federalists would get a nasty surprise.

The rain poured down. The men worked. Only a shaft of light from the lighthouse on La Bufa, the hill guarding the northern approaches to the city, could pierce the utter blackness; and that, for only a little distance. Then its rays too dissolved into the rainy dark.

Midmorning, as the mists lifted, the newly moved *Villista* artillery burst into a roar that shook the hillside, and the battle was begun.

Enemy guns had been aimed to pummel the *Villista* emplacements—but these had been abandoned in the night. Federalist shells burst harmlessly where cannon no longer stood, while Revolutionary soldiers swarmed up the hills, too close to be hit by the Federalist cannon fire.

Mobile artillery boomed out the advance of other *Villista* units from other directions. The hills resounded. "Señor!" thought Villa. "How sweet these cannon sound when they're firing on the enemy!"

Abruptly, all too close, there was a terrible blast, and when the smoke cleared, it appeared that a shell, which a Villa soldier had been trying to load, had burst, killing a number of men in the near vicinity and terrifying the others. Villa moved quickly among them, reassuring them. ". . . I'm here with you. I'll protect you." And Angeles reiterated his earlier order: "Fire without interruption!"

By noon the Revolutionaries' flag had appeared on one hilltop after another. In the early afternoon, Federalist fire, which had begun to diminish, burst out in fresh fury, and Villa was awed at the courage with which men who already knew they were defeated could go on fighting.

As the sun was going down the last important hill, *El Grillo*, "The Cricket," fell; and Federalist soldiers were fleeing the town by every route.

But the escape routes were blocked; Villa's cannons covered every canyon, every pass. By the time dark fell, not more than a few hundred Federalist soldiers had escaped; the others were dead, wounded or captured. It was a battle that would spell the end of the dictatorship of Victoriano Huerta.

Villa's victory, however, was probably more infuriating to Carranza than a defeat might have been. The First Chief was quick to take his revenge. He stripped Felipe Angeles of his post in the Constitutionalist cabinet. When Villa asked for fresh supplies of coal for his "rolling stock," to be used in

Revolution Rekindled

an attack on Aguascalientes, farther south, Carranza refused him; and Villa's trains could not move out of the Zacatecas rail yards. The First Chief prevented delivery of ammunition which Villa had ordered and paid for. And worst of all, he promoted Obregón and Pablo González to division generals; but left Villa's rank at that of brigadier, which it had been all along.

Privately, Villa raged at the injustice, but he kept silent; and when Pablo González called a conference in Torreón, to try to reconcile Villa's and Carranza's difficulties, Villa went.

The conference, however, was a failure. Compromises suggested by Carranza's own delegates were summarily rejected by the First Chief. He refused to reach any agreement with Villa; and, more ominously, refused to take any public position on land distribution for the peasants or on the rights of workers. And he flatly refused to guarantee a free election. What kind of revolutionary leader was this?

Meanwhile, Obregón's army had been pressing down the sultry, rainswept Pacific coast; he had then turned inland, and taken Guadalajara, the second largest city in Mexico. A little more than two hundred miles to the east, Pablo González had been preparing an attack on Querétaro. These drives were to have been part of the "grand triumphal march" on Mexico City which Villa had dreamed of for the three great armies. Instead, while the other two continued their victories en route the capital, Villa found himself powerless, his trains immobilized at Zacatecas.

What to do? Well—it had been a long, hard campaign; perhaps a little rest and pleasure wouldn't hurt. Tomás Urbina had expropriated an *hacienda* in Durango a while back; now he invited his old friend to Las Nieves for his baby's christening, and Villa made up his mind to go.

He paused at Parral, along the way, and found it moist

and green after the summer's rains. The welcome he was given by the townspeople, and by his old friend Maclovio Herrera, warmed his heart; and he went on to Las Nieves in a happier frame of mind.

The fiesta at Urbina's *hacienda* went on for days. In the central compound, as big as a city block, there were cockfights, and dances, and barbecues; the army band Villa had brought with him played army songs, and waltzes; and, of course, the baby was christened. Also, because Villa did not drink, Urbina himself drank less than usual, which was fortunate; in his cups, the "Lion of Durango" was likely to get bloodthirsty, and several times had even tried to shoot his mother—a sign of affection, the townspeople said. Instead, now there were long nostalgic talks between the two former outlaws. Villa could almost forget about the two armies not his own which were racing for the capital.

Just before he left, Urbina took him aside privately, and warned him to beware of Carranza. "Be ready for the break, my friend," he said. "Carranza is waiting to annihilate you."

On July 15th, as the surviving Federalist troops were moving southward in ragged retreat before the oncoming Revolutionaries, Victoriano Huerta bowed to the inevitable. He turned the government over to a provisional President, Francisco Carvajal, and five days later set sail from Veracruz for Europe and exile, as so many Mexican despots had done before him.

Three weeks later the acting President resigned too, and slipped quietly off to Veracruz. On August 10th, 1914, the Federalist garrisons in Mexico City surrendered; and on the 15th, Alvaro Obregón entered the capital with his troops.

When he had first joined the Revolution, most of Obregón's soldiers had come from his native coastlands of Sonora —Mayo Indians, who fought with bows and arrows. Since then, they had been joined by other Indians, the Yaqui, who had good reason to hate the government's army. The two tribal groups entered Mexico City pounding their Indian drums in ancient rhythms, with Obregón's infantry and cavalry marching before and aft. It was an eerie blend of past and present.

Obregón marched to the *Zócalo* at the head of his troops and, from the balcony of the National Palace overlooking the great square below, took formal possession of the city in the name of Venustiano Carranza.

Five days later, Carranza made his own triumphal entry —mounted, equestrian that he was, on a magnificent black horse. He led a procession along the Paseo de la Reforma to the *Zócalo;* and in the National Palace, which had seen so many rulers come and go, announced that he would preside, officially, as "First Chief of the Executive Power."

PART FIVE

Turmoil

CHAPTER 20

WHILE CARRANZA WAS settling into his new post in Mexico City, fighting had broken out in Sonora. It was an old quarrel between the *Villista* governor José María Maytorena on one side, and the *Carrancista* generals Benjamín Hill and Plutarco Elías Calles on the other, over control of the state.

Carranza was trying to maintain a show of unity among his generals. He knew Maytorena would be responsive to Villa's requests, and accordingly, ordered Alvaro Obregón north, to ask Villa to intercede in the matter. Obregón—amiable, practical, and always ready to work for the good of the Revolution—promptly set out by train for Chihuahua.

He left behind him a city little changed from the days of Huerta's rule. Early in Carranza's reign, a new verb was coined: *carrancear*, meaning "to steal."

The First Chief himself was far too upright to do the stealing; but his flatterers and hangers-on were another matter. They requisitioned and moved into the houses of wealthy residents, and helped themselves to everything that was movable. Banks were systematically looted—by official order. Fortunes were made overnight.

And if there were any dreamers who had hopes of social change under Carranza's Constitutionalist government, they were quickly disillusioned. The First Chief made no move toward distribution of land to the peasants. When workers asked for better wages and housing, he did not seem to hear them. He printed more paper money, and living costs soared. There was no mention of an election.

And though Villa was still technically his ally, Carranza's police were rounding up dozens of Villa's supporters in Mexico City and elsewhere, and holding them without charges in Lecumberri prison in the capital.

One such captive was Martín Luis Guzmán, a talented young journalist who had been traveling with Villa's army, and who would one day edit Villa's memoirs. Guzmán, though attracted by Villa's impulsive warmth and directness, was no blind adherent of the former outlaw. Dealing with him, he would later admit, was like handling dynamite. He stated the problem clearly: "Either Villa would submit to the principles of the Revolution, in which case he and the Revolution would triumph. Or he would follow his own blind impulses, and he and the Revolution would go down to defeat."

But those words would not appear for more than a decade. Obregón, on the train for Chihuahua in August, 1914, was about to discover for himself what it was like to be in Pancho Villa's orbit.

At first, all went well. Villa met him at the station and greeted him cordially. They went to Villa's house, and had a long and friendly discussion; Villa opened his heart to the ex-farmer from Sonora, pouring out his grievances toward Carranza and his fears for the fate of the Revolution. A day or two after Obregón's arrival, they set out by train for Sonora, with Villa, now filled with warmth for his big, good-natured guest, calling him *compañerito*, "little friend."

In Sonora, the two men arranged a truce of sorts between

Turmoil

the opposing parties, and returned to Chihuahua, Villa still calling Obregón his *compañerito*. At Villa's urging, they drew up a petition to Carranza, asking him to set up a proper interim government, with cabinet, judges, and machinery for local governments; and to make arrangements for national elections for senators and deputies. To all appearances, the visit could not have been more harmonious.

Unfortunately, when Obregón returned to the capital and presented the petition to Carranza, the First Chief simply laid it aside. All such matters, he said, would be referred to a convention he was calling for the first of October.

However, something was achieved. On the strength of Obregón's request, Carranza promoted Villa to divisional general.

But no sooner was the trouble in Sonora quieted, than similar skirmishes broke out in Durango, and once more Obregón took the train north to visit Villa and try to work out a solution. At least, that was his overt reason for returning.

Actually, when he had left Chihuahua earlier, Villa had seemed ready to support Carranza. But since then, the tone of Villa's telegrams had turned abruptly hostile; and Obregón felt it would be wise to go back and find out what had happened.

This time, Villa's reception of him was more chilling. It was the *diez-y-seis*, the sixteenth of September; and Villa treated his guest to a three-hour Independence Day parade. As thousands of footsoldiers, cavalry, artillerymen—with their weapons—marched past the reviewing stand, Obregón was well aware of the implied threat. Villa even took him to a warehouse and showed him the vast amount of ammunition stored there.

Then, there was Villa's manner—no longer open and friendly as it had been before; rather, the "Centaur of the

North" was controlled, almost ominously quiet, as though waiting for Obregón to make a slip.

Obregón was not surprised, then, to be summoned suddenly to Villa's house next day and to find Villa livid with rage. His extraordinary amber-colored eyes, always bloodshot from sun and wind, were now mere angry slits; as they glared at Obregón they almost seemed to dart fire. Furiously, Villa accused Obregón of treachery in the Sonora business. Fighting had broken out there again, and it was Obregón's doing, he charged.

Obregón denied responsibility, but Villa was too angry to listen. Peremptorily he summoned his elite guard, his *dorados*; and when they appeared, the gold braid of their uniforms gleaming, he ordered them to take the Sonoran out to the courtyard and shoot him.

Shocked, Obregón managed to retain his composure. Villa had always been known for his sudden rages. As an outlaw, he had spent his youth wary of betrayals, shooting his way out of ambushes; later, as a soldier, he had suffered from the treacheries of turncoats like Pascual Orozco and Victoriano Huerta. By now he had an almost paranoidal fear of betrayal, and his hand was never far from his pistol.

Too, as Obregón had been told by Villa's secretary "Luisito" Aguirre Benavides, Villa's moods often depended on which of his advisers he had been listening to: the calm, wise Felipe Angeles, or the hotheaded, bloodthirsty duo Rodolfo Fierro and Tomás Urbina. It was clear whom he had been listening to today.

Obregón faced Villa quietly. "If you shoot me now," he said, "you'll be doing me a favor and yourself harm. Because I joined the Revolution ready to die for it; it would only bring me glory. While if you shoot me, it would cost you your honor."

Villa was too angry to care. There was a crowd in the room now. Along with the *dorados*, Villa's followers had be-

Turmoil

gun to push into the room, and some of Obregón's staff; all were tense, afraid to speak. When Villa repeated his angry order for the execution, someone's voice suddenly broke the silence. "Bravo!" it cried out. "That's the way to do it!"

Everyone's head turned. It was Villa's staff doctor, jumping up and down with excitement. He had once been dismissed by Obregón, and had reason to hate him.

Villa whirled on him. Calling him an idiot, he ordered him from the room. But the incident seemed to have deflected his rage, and as one of Obregón's staff members moved to his side and began to speak to him in a quiet, persuasive tone, Villa—still breathing heavily—listened. The man spoke of Villa's bravery and honor, and told him he had too much of both to kill a man who was a guest in his house. Better, he said, if the two adversaries were out on the field, shooting it out between them.

Villa knew he had almost shot the doctor over one foolish word; he must not shoot Obregón now in the same blind rage, when he was not even capable of thinking clearly.

He had to get away, be alone, until he was calm again . . .

Without a word, he left the room.

Everyone waited.

In half an hour he sent in an order for the *dorados* to be withdrawn. In another half-hour he dismissed the guards who held Obregón captive. Finally he came back to the room, sat Obregón down on the sofa beside him, and said, with tears in his eyes, "Francisco Villa is not an assassin, or a traitor, señor. But in trying to help Carranza, don't deceive me. Don't even let it *look* as though you're deceiving me!"

Then he threw his arm around Obregón, called him *compañerito* again, and took him into the dining room for dinner.

Next day, the two reconciled leaders drafted a letter to Venustiano Carranza, accepting his invitation to the conference of October 1st, and Obregón started back to Mexico City.

But halfway to Torreón, the train was halted. Obregón's escort had received orders to bring him back to Chihuahua. Villa had discovered that Carranza—hearing rumors in Mexico City that Obregón had been shot—had ordered the destruction of the railroad tracks below Zacatecas, and an attack on Villa if he should try to come farther south.

Immediately, Villa had publicly denounced Carranza; and when Obregón had arrived in Chihuahua and was brought before him again, the whole tragic comedy was played out once more: Obregón stood calm and controlled before Villa's rage, and was once more condemned to be shot.

This time it was the more temperate of Villa's advisers who dissuaded their chief from the rash act; and once more Obregón was put aboard the train for the capital. But by the time he was halfway there Villa had been convinced again by his trigger-happy friends that Obregón was indeed a traitor, and had sent out still another order for his arrest and execution.

By pure luck, however, the train was not stopped, and Obregón reached Mexico City—shaken, but alive.

Villa's public disavowal of Carranza cost him several adherents. Some he could shrug off. But when he received a letter from his old *compadre* Maclovio Herrera, denouncing him for the act and rejecting him as a leader and friend, he wept.

There would be other such losses in the future—losses of friends, losses of honor. But right now, for Villa, the most important matter was to make sure that that old badger Venustiano Carranza did not destroy the Revolution.

CHAPTER 21

THE CONVENTION CALLED by Carranza was all but ignored by most of the Revolutionaries. It was superceded by another, called for October 5th, to be held in neutral territory—about halfway between Villa's Zacatecas and Carranza's Mexico City, in the pleasant little agricultural town of Aguascalientes. For a country already weary of war, it was a last hope for peace.

The rainy season was just ending, leaving the hills and fields moist and green, as were the town's countless little plazas. The air was fresh and clear, the streets gay with banners welcoming the delegates. And, to make sure there would be no drunken incidents to shatter the harmony, all the *cantinas* were shut down.

The delegates met in a theater to one side of the main plaza. The generals sat onstage, amid the smell of dust and grease paint, with flats and backdrops stacked in the wings and ropes looped overhead. Other delegates sat in the audience or in the boxes; and Antonio I. Villareal, a staunch *Maderista* who had spent three years in California jails for publishing an anti-Díaz newspaper there, presided. The prime mover, however, was Alvaro Obregón.

As for Villa—he had sent an envoy to represent him, twenty-nine-year-old Roque González Garza. But in case the Convention bred not peace but war, he had moved eleven thousand of his troops down to Guadalupe, a village near Zacatecas about a hundred miles north of the Convention site. Here, living in his special railroad car, as he always did in the field, he waited, to see how things went.

Equally cautious, Carranza's General Pablo González was encamped with *his* forces two hundred and fifty miles southeast of Villa, where he could make a quick move if Villa did.

Venustiano Carranza refused to attend.

Nor would Emiliano Zapata participate, until Felipe Angeles was sent to the valley of Morelos, to seek him out in his hideaway among the protective hills, and persuade him to send a delegation.

The Convention's first act was to declare its sovereignty as supreme governing force of Mexico. When Carranza received news of this in Mexico City, he denied they had any such right; he himself was still First Chief. Nevertheless, the delegates in Aguascalientes went ahead to chart a course for the beleaguered republic.

Within the first few days, González Garza gave a speech on Villa's behalf, pledging Villa's support of the Convention, and stating his leader's aims for free elections, a just land distribution, and laws to protect the poor. The speech was well-received, and a few days later, Villa himself was sent for.

Villa's private life, at that moment, was troubled. Used to easy romantic conquests, he found himself being steadily rejected by a well-brought-up young woman he had taken a fancy to. She met all his advances with tears, which baffled him and hurt his self-esteem. Too, he had received word that the *Carrancista* general, Pablo González, had sent a man to try to assassinate him—further proof that you couldn't trust anyone.

However, in response to the Convention's summons, he came to Aguascalientes, and appeared at the Teatro Morelos.

Villa was never at ease in such awesome surroundings. He had squeezed his barrel-chested body into his best uniform, and even tried to wet down and smooth his rebellious curly hair. He came awkwardly down the aisle, aware as never before of his *campesino* manner, his lack of education. But from all sides of him came shouts of "*Viva* Villa!" and, somewhat emboldened, he mounted the stage and spoke.

"*Compañeritos,* generals and officials . . ." he began. "You're going to hear the words of a man who comes before you as uncultured as the day he was born. But if there are men of conscience here, who have an understanding of one's duty to one's country—I'll try not to make them ashamed of me."

He sought nothing for himself, he said. All he wanted was the welfare of the people and the relief of the poor. "I say only this. I want a bright future for my country, because I have suffered much for it, and I don't want my fellow countrymen to go through what I've gone through, or to suffer what I've seen women and children suffer in these mountains, and on these fields, and on these *haciendas* . . ."

He was crying as he spoke, but couldn't help himself. "The future of the country is in your hands," he went on. "The destiny of all of us Mexicans. And if it's lost, it will be your responsibility—yours, you men of law and intelligence!"

Alvaro Obregón moved to his side and enveloped him in a huge *abrazo,* while the audience leaped cheering to its feet. Then Villa signed the Mexican flag which stood beside him, as the other delegates had done, and took his oath of loyalty to the Convention.

The attitude of the delegates toward Venustiano Carranza, however, was another matter. One night soon after, while films were shown of the early days of the Revolution, Carranza's image was flashed on the screen, and the theater filled with boos and hisses. When he was shown on his handsome black horse riding into Mexico City, one of the onlookers excitedly fired two shots at him—the bullets ripping through the screen and burying themselves in the brick wall at the back of the stage.

Meanwhile, delegates from Zapata arrived—peasant-soldiers, in their *huaraches* (sandals) and white cotton pants and shirts; and a couple of spokesmen more formally dressed in embroidered *charro* suits and wide-brimmed, embroidered *charro* hats. One such colorfully dressed delegate, Antonio Soto y Gama, spoke for Zapata, demanding that the Convention accept Zapata's "Plan of Ayala"—the document drawn up early in Madero's reign, calling for land for the peasants. In passionate terms he accused the Convention of being a conference of generals, and at one point, grabbed up the flag which had been signed by all the delegates, and called it a "dyed rag, bedaubed with the image of a bird of prey [the Mexican eagle]!" The audience rose almost as a man, yelling invective and pulling out their pistols. Most of them, it seemed, came armed to these peace conferences.

Then, notice arrived from Carranza, stating that he would resign his post and recognize the rule of the Convention—only if both Villa and Zapata relinquished their armies and left the country.

Here at last, just as it looked as though the Convention were coming apart at the seams, lay a possible compromise. While such a resolution was being drafted, the delegates set about to decide on a candidate for provisional President of the country. Their choice was Eulalio Gutiérrez.

Gutiérrez was a short-necked, heavy-set man who had been a train-dynamiter in the early days of the Revolution. He was earnest, deeply devoted to the Revolution, and had no personal ambition. The primary reason he was chosen, however, was that he was completely neutral: he was not attached to any of the contending military leaders.

When Villa received from Gutiérrez a proposal that he and Carranza resign and leave the country, he agreed immediately. He went further. He suggested that for the sake of future peace, both he and Carranza face a firing squad.

The delegates rejected the offer, and Villa lost his chance at martyrdom for his country. Instead, he merely resigned his commission, as the delegates asked, and waited for Carranza to do the same.

Carranza, however, wired the Convention that he had *not* resigned, and did not recognize Gutiérrez as President —nor would he, until Villa had left the country. He left the palace in Mexico City, and moved with his staff toward Veracruz, whence he could attack or ship out, depending on subsequent developments. He conferred with Pablo González and other military leaders who were still faithful to him, and moved quickly from town to town, to avoid having to talk to the Convention's envoys. Finally he sent another wire stating that any generals supporting the Convention were guilty of treason.

For Eulalio Gutiérrez, there was no alternative. He declared Carranza to be in a "state of rebellion," and ordered Zapata's forces to move northeast in an attack on the First Chief's forces.

Villa, who had admired Zapata's guerrilla technique in the hills and valleys of Morelos, had his doubts about the chances of those barefoot, cotton-clad peasants against Carranza's formidable army. Nevertheless, his own way was clear. He sent Zapata a wire saying, "The hour has come. In the morning I begin my march to the capital"; and began to move his troops against Pablo González's encampment at Querétaro.

Three armies were now on the move. The peace was broken.

In the meantime, Obregón had gone north to seek out Carranza. He finally caught up with him, and there was a long—and fateful—discussion. At the end of it, Obregón came back to Mexico City with his decision made.

The ex-farmer from the Sonora coastlands, intimately acquainted with the very soil he had been fighting for these last four or five years, did nothing rashly, ever. He had a powerful army, and had proved himself a brilliant general, but he would not use his military advantage to promote himself. The time had come when he must throw his strength behind whichever man would serve his country best.

It had been a choice between hotheaded, uncontrollable Pancho Villa, who was even now sweeping south toward the capital with his irresistible army, and Venustiano Carranza—wily, vain, dictatorial, but far more predictable, and probably, in the long run, stronger. Too, Obregón had had, only weeks before, a taste of Villa's mercurial temper; it did not bode well for future peace.

He had decided to support Carranza.

In return, the First Chief appointed Obregón his chief of operations. On November 19th, 1914, Obregón issued a declaration of war against Pancho Villa.

On November 23rd, United States troops—which had been occupying the harbor of Veracruz all this time—withdrew. But in the excitement of reopened hostilities throughout Mexico, the act was hardly noted.

What had happened? How could the Convention, which had begun with such promise, prove such a failure?

The young journalist Martín Luis Guzmán, now released from jail and present in Aguascalientes through most of the Convention, hazarded a guess. He said of the delegates, "It was not the Revolution they were fighting for, but its spoils." And none of the leaders would surrender his chance at the lion's share.

Obregón did not yet have his forces organized to their fullest strength, and knew that the four thousand troops he had on hand in the capital could not hope to defend it. On the twenty-fourth of November, he withdrew. Lucio Blanco, the colorful and talented general who had served under Pablo González but whose loyalties were now a mystery, took over the city with his fifteen thousand men. He was in charge for two days; then he too withdrew, with his men, toward safer ground in the west.

Villa and his *División del Norte*—which had now become the "Army of the Convention"—were moving inexorably closer to the capital, defeating *Carrancista* troops at Querétaro, and taking smaller towns one after another along the way.

But the first to fill the vacuum, the first truly revolutionary army to reach Mexico City, were the peasant-soldiers from the valley of Morelos—the men of Emiliano Zapata.

CHAPTER 22

ZAPATA PAUSED AT the south end of the city where, in case of need, he would have quick access to the mountains which separated the valley of Mexico from his own valley of Morelos. He stationed most of his men at Xochimilco, the "floating gardens" of the Aztecs' time—tree-shaded canals along which fruits and flowers were floated in dug-out canoes to the Mexico City markets. Other units were stationed at Mixcoac, and in the quiet colonial village of San Angel.

Most of his peasant army had never seen the city and were awed and intimidated by it. To the residents' surprise, there was no looting, no violence; instead, the white-clad, sandaled or barefoot men went timidly from door to door, asking for food, and astonished the devout by wearing Guadalupe medals and attending Mass.

But Villa's trains were on the way, and his *División del Norte* troops would be a different story.

On December 2nd, the trains rolled into the city from the northwest, and Villa set up headquarters at Tacuba. He put Felipe Angeles in charge of military discipline, and gave orders that anyone disturbing the public order was to be

Turmoil 153

shot. His men had wreaked havoc after the battle of Zacatecas; it must not happen here in the capital.

His next move was to set up a conference with Emiliano Zapata.

On December 4th, he and a few members of his staff rode their horses the twenty-odd miles across the city to Zapata's headquarters. As they dismounted and started toward the tiny two-story village schoolhouse, Zapata came out to meet them—slight, dark-faced, with the deep-set black eyes of his Indian forebears. It was an emotional meeting; the local band played Revolutionary songs: "La Cucaracha," which the *Villista* soldiers had sung in camp and on top of railroad cars all over northern Mexico; the *Zapatistas*' "Valentina," and even the *Carrancistas*' tender, sorrowful "Las Adelitas"—making up in enthusiasm what they lacked in skill; and the townspeople showered the two groups with more flowers than they could carry.

When at last the two leaders could speak to each other alone, they agreed that their two armies would cooperate; and Villa promised Zapata arms and ammunition if he needed them. They agreed there should be a civilian President; and each mentioned the names of a few men, attached to the other's camp, who for the good of the Revolution should be executed. Then, rejoining their followers, they settled down to a huge *ranchero* meal. Villa even managed to choke down a few sips of *pulque*, something he wouldn't have done for anyone in Mexico except Emiliano Zapata.

Two days later there was a triumphal parade, Villa entering Mexico City from the north and Zapata from the south, until the two armies converged; watchers estimated the joint forces at almost fifty thousand men. Then they marched to the Zócalo, where Eulalio Gutiérrez—who had by now reached the city—feasted the two chiefs at the National Palace.

It was a photographers' field day. After dinner the newsmen trailed the presidential party about the palace, to the accompaniment of bursts of flash powder and the click of big box cameras. When they reached the Room of State, with its formal decor and expensive hangings, the photographers persuaded Villa to sit in the presidential chair.

He complied. But he was clearly uncomfortable, and made his escape from it as soon as the pictures were taken. Whatever his enemies may have been saying about him, the President's chair was not his goal.

These winter days in the capital should have been a proud time for Villa—the culmination of his long, hard drive down from the north. He was trying consciously to prove his loyalty and usefulness to the Convention and President Gutiérrez. But Mexico City was not like a battlefield, where friend and enemy were cleanly divided, and where all one needed was a clear plan of battle and enough men, ammunition, and courage. Here, nothing was simple or clear-cut. One behaved as one had always done in the field—but things kept turning out badly . . .

For instance, his efforts to keep order in the city. Even his summary justice ("Try them tonight and shoot them in the morning!") could not keep the riotous *norteños* in control; their occupation grew more violent day by day. As for Villa's old friend Tomás Urbina—the former outlaw prowled from one rich house to the next, exacting forced "loans" from the inhabitants, who never knew if the money went for the support of his troops, or for the upkeep of his *hacienda* at Las Nieves.

Then there was the matter of young David Berlanga, an officer with the Conventionalists, and a lawyer and teacher. One night in a downtown restaurant he had become angry at a group of drunken *Villistas* who refused to pay their check. Denouncing the *División del Norte* as a bunch of bandits, he paid their bill himself. Villa, hearing of the incident and infuriated by the insult to his army, ordered his "butcher" Rodolfo Fierro to find Berlanga and shoot him.

Fierro tracked him down the next night at the same restaurant. Having finished his dinner, Berlanga was smoking a good cigar. When Fierro told him he was under arrest, the young man rose calmly, paid his bill, and followed Fierro out to his car—taking care not to drop the long, glowing ash from his cigar.

What happened subsequently so upset the ruthless Fierro that he sought out Martín Luis Guzmán—by now Assistant Secretary of War—and told him the story, as though looking for some sort of forgiveness.

Berlanga had gone with him to the guardhouse, said Fierro, and there, still calm, rapidly scribbled a note. This, together with everything in his pockets, he asked Fierro to deliver to his mother. Then he told his executioner that he was ready, and they went together out into the dark courtyard where a group of Villa's *dorados* were waiting, with their rifles. He was still smoking; the ever lengthening ash of his cigar was still intact. Fierro indicated the bullet-pocked wall; and Berlanga nodded, promising not to keep him waiting.

He continued smoking the cigar a moment or two longer; then, abruptly, flicked off the ash, discarded the cigar butt and ground it out with his boot. He refused to let his eyes be bandaged, nor would he turn his back on the firing squad, but stood facing them in complete calm, until the volley was fired.

Fierro, as he told the story to Guzmán, had been pulling at a cigar of his own, nervously. "Look," he said to the young man. "Since early this morning I've been trying to smoke a cigar without letting the ash fall, but it's no use."

He could not keep his fingers from twitching, and the ash would fall . . .

Villa himself did not indulge in gunfights in the streets, nor was he ever guilty of drunkenness—but he did very nearly draw Mexico into an international scandal by pressing his attentions on a pretty young cashier in a French-owned hotel. It was all the Gutiérrez government could do to get charges of kidnaping withdrawn.

In fact, Gutiérrez and many of his cabinet members were growing seriously disenchanted with Villa and his army; and Gutiérrez had begun, cautiously, to look for a way out of his dilemma. He was wise to be cautious: Villa had ordered the execution of a hundred and fifty political "enemies" in his first three weeks in the capital.

The country at large was riven by factions now. The *Villista* governor of Sonora, José María Maytorena, was still fighting the two *Carrancista* generals over control of the state, and there had been incursions onto American soil; some of the exploding shells had cost the lives of American nationals across the border, and damaged American property. On Mexico's east coast, Obregón was in possession of much of the territory between Puebla and Veracruz, and other *Carrancistas* held most of the Isthmus of Tehuantepec, to the southeast. The loyalty of Lucio Blanco and other generals in the central part of the country was an open question. The Revolution had become, as one historian put it, "one grand dogfight."

On December 12th, however, Carranza—persuaded by his more liberal followers—issued a statement that made it possible for many of the more radical Revolutionaries to support him at last. He urged a program of land redistribution, social justice, and labor and tax reforms. In the same statement he included a bitter denunciation of Villa as a "reactionary."

Villa contemplated the statement wryly. "While he was accusing me of reaction," he wrote later, "he was paying me the compliment of adopting my program!"

He did not realize how much support Carranza's statement would call forth, nor how much his own hot-tempered excesses would cost him in friends and allies—including Eulalio Gutiérrez. When he heard in late December that the President was planning to dismiss him and leave the capital, he was outraged; and set off, pistol in hand, to accost Gutiérrez in his house.

Gutiérrez was frank. He wanted subordinates, he said, who would obey him and respect the law. In short, "I want to be as far away as possible from you and Emiliano Zapata," he said. "I don't want to feel responsible any longer for the crimes your men commit in the name of my government!"

Villa, still barely able to keep his rage in check, said he would not let Gutiérrez go. He, Villa, had stopped all the trains.

"I'd leave on a mule," said the President, "if it would get me away from you."

Villa responded furiously that he was there to protect Gutiérrez, and there were two thousand *Villista* troops outside right now to prove it. Gutiérrez looked out his window and saw that his house was encircled. "So now you know, señor!" said Villa. "You may want to get away from me, but you're not leaving this house!"

Having made a virtual prisoner of the President, Villa felt secure enough to go north to the border, soon after the beginning of 1915, to confer with two American officials with whom he had been friendly throughout his campaigns. The problem, of course, was the Mexican bullets which were costing American lives across the border from the fighting in Sonora.

At the talks, he agreed to urge his ally, General Maytorena, to seek a settlement; and started back, making stops at Chihuahua and Torreón.

But the situation countrywide was changing rapidly. He had received word on the way that Zapata's men, having captured the historic town of Puebla, had lost it again to Alvaro Obregón. Elsewhere, Rodolfo Fierro was once more trying to drive the *Carrancistas* out of Guadalajara. And Villa's chief of operations Felipe Angeles was battling Maclovio Herrera's forces all along the railroad to the east, in Coahuila and Nuevo León.

The news from Angeles continued to be good. He and his men took Saltillo, and then occupied the important industrial city of Monterrey without opposition.

En route, however, his men had seized correspondence from the defeated *Carrancistas* which proved beyond all doubt that Gutiérrez was planning to turn against those "bandits and criminals": Villa and Zapata.

Nor was that the worst of it. From other letters which Angeles forwarded to Villa, it was clear that many more of Villa's friends and former allies were planning to support Gutiérrez in the action—among them Minister of War José Isabel Robles; the hard-fighting General Lucio Blanco; and, more worrisome, Eugenio Aguirre Benavides—brother of "Luisito," who had been Villa's secretary since the battle of Tierra Blanca more than a year ago. Villa, shaken by these mass defections, was suddenly apprehensive about Luisito, whom he had been genuinely fond of. The boy was in Mexico City now; would he, too, desert him, as his older brother had done?

Hurt, angry, he started back for the capital, but was barely on his way when he heard that some time during the early dawn of January 16th, Eulalio Gutiérrez and his cabinet had slipped out of Mexico City, taking with them some ten million pesos of the national treasury.

Within two days came more bad news. Rodolfo Fierro

Turmoil

and his fellow commander had suffered a severe defeat at Guadalajara; even now, survivors of the battle, both well and wounded, were entrained and on their way north to safety.

Villa was furious. Now, when he needed all his strength to track down Gutiérrez, and to fight the Obregón and Carranza forces in the east, he must drop everything and retake Guadalajara. How could Fierro be so stupid!

He was in Aguascalientes one evening, waiting for Fierro's arrival, to give him a piece of his mind, when he had an unexpected visitor. Martín Luis Guzmán had just come in on the mail train from Mexico City and was waiting for him outside his caboose.

Villa had liked this sober young idealist—who, like Luisito, had also joined him soon after the battle of Tierra Blanca. The boy had known Obregón and Carranza, but had chosen to ally himself with Villa. He was brilliantly educated, and deeply devoted to the principles of the Revolution.

Now Villa greeted him with his warmest *abrazo*, lifting him clear off the ground. He took him into the sitting room of the caboose and threw questions at him. What was all this about "Ulalio" slipping out of Mexico City? And what did Guzmán think about those dirty turncoats Benavides and Robles? And Luisito—even Luisito was leaving him! But Guzmán would take his place, said Villa. "From now on, you're going to stay right here with me. I'm going to fix up Luisito's room for you. You'll be my secretary . . ."

There was a fraction of a second's pause. Then Guzmán asked if he could go, first, to look for his family up at the frontier, and find out if they were all right.

For a moment Villa looked straight into the young man's face, trying to read his eyes. Then he said, "You want to desert me too?"

Guzmán tried to answer and couldn't. Villa went on, "Don't desert me, my friend—because, believe me, I *am* your friend." There was another pause. "You're not going to desert me, are you?"

Then, quickly, before Guzmán could answer, Villa offered him money for the trip and a special train.

Two weeks later, Villa received a letter from him, postmarked El Paso.

"Señor general Villa," it read. "I am now on United States soil, where I have also found my family. I want to separate myself from the war. You must believe, my general, that when we said goodbye in Aguascalientes, I had no intention of deceiving you. I was sincere in my promise to come back, to be at your side in the moment of triumph.

"But I have come to realize that all the men I respect are now your enemies: Lucio Blanco is your enemy, my general, and José Isabel Robles, and Eulalio Gutiérrez, and Antonio I. Villareal; and I no more want to fight against them than I want to fight against you. Moreover, this new fight is no longer a fight for our cause, which was to overthrow Victoriano Huerta, but a fight over who shall control the government. I want to tell you, señor, that I am going far away from our homeland. I am going to countries where my acts cannot be viewed as hostile either to you or to the rest of my friends. And when I make this sacrifice, please understand the spirit of loyalty in which I have separated myself from all groups.

         Martín Luis Guzmán."

Villa read, and then reread the letter, with the same sense of loss and bewilderment he had felt so often lately. "Señor!" he asked himself, baffled. "Am I protecting the people's cause so badly that everyone has to abandon me?"

But there was no one to answer him.

PART SIX

Defeats

CHAPTER 23

THE FULL IMPACT of his losses, however, did not strike Villa yet; he was still winning a few battles, and could not know that 1915, for him, would prove the beginning of the end. Matters in Mexico City were still confusing. Villa's friend and ally, Roque González Garza, declared himself acting President; but worried by the steady approach of Obregón's forces from the north, had moved his government down to Cuernavaca, in Zapata's valley of Morelos. The end of January, Obregón and his ten thousand troops entered the capital, to find it desolate indeed: the *Zapatistas* had wrecked the city's pumps as they had withdrawn and there was no running water. All civil services were suspended—there was no mail service, and no telegraph. There was no public transportation, and no fuel for automobiles.

As the winter weeks wore away, things got worse. The cold was bitter; men chopped down trees in the parks and along the streets to get firewood for their stoves. Food distribution broke down; people began to suffer from hunger, though foodstuffs grown in the rich coastal areas around Veracruz were sold abroad to provide money for Carranza's army.

Word reached Villa that Obregón would do nothing toward solving these problems because he felt the city had been hostile to Carranza. Whatever the reason, the situation grew daily worse. The people of the city trapped rats for food. Many of them died of starvation on the streets, and among the living, disease became rampant. That year would become known, in the future, as "the year of hunger."

There were, now, four governments functioning simultaneously in Mexico as a whole: the Carranza-Obregón government in Mexico City and Veracruz; the government of Eulalio Gutiérrez, currently traveling from town to town northwest of the capital and as yet without a headquarters; what was left of Roque González Garza's Conventionalists, in combination with the *Zapatistas*; and Villa's newly established authority in the north-central areas.

As for the military situation, it was hard to know who was winning and who was losing. Of the *Villista* forces, Felipe Angeles was being threatened in Monterrey by Pablo González, and was writing Villa urgent requests for troop support. Tomás Urbina was driving toward the rich oil fields of Tampico. But Villa could help neither of them because he needed every man he could get for a new attack on Guadalajara.

In February of 1915 he began his move. He sent his men to Jalisco, the "Texas of Mexico," to points east, south, and west of Guadalajara; from there, they would converge on the city—which he hoped would be quickly evacuated by the enemy.

He proved correct. His troops, moving on the city from three directions, sent the *Carrancistas* fleeing before a major battle could be mounted. Villa paused no more than a day or two in the pleasant little metropolis before he was on the road again, determined to give the retreating enemy no rest. He caught up with them on the slopes of the sierra about a hundred miles south, at Cerro de Sayula, and defeated them badly. Then, leaving Fierro and two or three other generals in charge of the newly won territory, he returned north to help Felipe Angeles at Monterrey.

On his arrival there, the besieging enemy took flight so precipitately that he could boast to Angeles, "You see, señor General? Those *Carrancistas* flee at the jingle of my spurs!"

His army, however, was now spread very thin indeed: from the westerly states of Jalisco and Michoacán all the way north to the Texas border; and they were engaged with the enemy on half-a-dozen fronts. Inevitably under such circumstances, bad news began to mingle with the good. Fierro was again losing much of the newly won ground in Jalisco—and several thousand soldiers as well, along with horses and supplies. To the east, Urbina's General Manuel Chao had been stopped on his march to Tampico; and—most serious of all—on March 10th, Obregón had marched his entire force out of Mexico City and was on his way to Querétaro, to challenge Pancho Villa himself.

Felipe Angeles, temporarily invalided—a horse had fallen on him—warned Villa against marching south to meet the Obregón advance. Block his road, he said, harass him—but don't be drawn away from the stronghold of Torreón. "Don't fall into his trap!" he urged. "Don't go south!"

But Villa was reckless, now, and filled with personal anger at the man who had wooed away so many of his old supporters. In earlier times he would have profited from Angeles's advice; now he scarcely heard it. He must engage Obregón quickly, he said, before Obregón's forces grew any stronger.

He hastened to outfit his troops, eight thousand of them to Obregón's twelve thousand. He would not even wait for the arrival of four of his generals whom he had ordered up from the fighting in Michoacán. Ammunition his brother

Hipólito had bought and paid for in the United States had not arrived, but even this could not deter him. All Villa could think of was that Obregón's men had taken Celaya and the towns nearby, and were assembling there; and it was his, Pancho Villa's, duty to attack them and, in one enormous blow, destroy them.

Obregón, in the meantime, had learned something new about battle technique. War had broken out the previous year in Europe, and German and Allied armies were using a new method of fortification: trenches and barbed wire. These were the defenses that had stopped Manuel Chao's advance toward the east coast; and here on the level wheatlands of Celaya, already crisscrossed with irrigation ditches, it was a natural means of defense.

Equally important, Obregón was receiving trainload after trainload of ammunition from Carranza, while Villa, advancing now from Irapuato, was drawing steadily farther from his centers of supply in the north.

On the morning of April 6th, Villa's forces threw themselves on Obregón's entrenchments just east of Celaya.

By five in the afternoon, Obregón's men had retreated to fortifications on the very outskirts of the city. Some of Villa's men even pushed them back into Celaya itself, but faced such heavy fire they were forced to withdraw. At night, Obregón's forces pulled back to the protection of the city, and Villa's to their own positions not far outside. Villa's chiefs were worried about a shortage of ammunition, but Villa was confident there would be enough; Celaya would fall, he assured them, in their first assault next day.

Fighting began again at four in the morning; by dawn the *División del Norte* was feeling the deadly effect of the rifle fire of Obregón's Yaqui soldiers. Horses of Villa's cavalry, trying to leap the trenches, were disemboweled by

Defeats

bayonet-wielding riflemen below, or hopelessly trapped in barbed wire. Villa was everywhere, urging his men on; but their every attack was pushed back. At last, with neither side able to claim a victory, Villa withdrew his exhausted troops, and marched them back to Irapuato.

There, he tried desperately to bolster his battered forces. He wired Urbina to finish the Tampico advance and come join him, but Urbina, Chao, and their men were still unable to get past the barbed-wire entrenchments at El Ebano. He sent for his troops from Jalisco. He sent off frantic wires to his brother Hipólito in Ciudad Juárez, demanding the promised ammunition; but because of difficulties with United States authorities at the border, Hipólito could obtain only a limited amount, and many of the cartridges he did send proved the wrong caliber for Villa's guns.

And in the meantime, while Villa was increasing the size of his striking force considerably, Obregón was doubling his.

On the morning of April 13th, the *Villistas* began assembling near Celaya. They took their positions and, in the late afternoon, opened their attack. They went into battle with eighteen cartridges apiece.

They fought through what was left of that afternoon, and all through the night. The second day the fighting continued without pause. The second night, rain poured down, and there was a few hours' respite; but by dawn the battle had resumed.

Since the battle had begun, Villa had wondered at the absence of Obregón's cavalry. Perhaps, he reasoned, they were all fighting as riflemen. Had he forgotten Obregón's classical technique—to let his enemy attack until exhausted, then strike a massive blow which would finish him? At midmorning of that third day, four thousand *Obregónista* cavalrymen, who had been hidden in the mesquite throughout the whole battle thus far, emerged suddenly from their hiding places and, with more than as many infantrymen, charged down on the *División del Norte.* It was a tragic slaughter.

Villa wanted to fight on. But too many of his units had lost their officers. Ammunition was almost exhausted, and such shells as he still had were defective. On all sides of him men were flinging down their rifles and scrambling out of the line of fire to safety. Wearily, he gave the order for retreat.

By nightfall, when he and his troops drew into sight of their trains at Salamanca, he was surprised—and infinitely relieved—to realize that the *Obregónistas* had not pursued them. He could not have withstood an attack. He had lost almost half his men.

Back in Aguascalientes, Felipe Angeles once again urged caution. But Villa would not acknowledge defeat. He was determined to fight Obregón to the finish.

This time, while he reorganized his shattered army, he allowed Obregón to advance northward. It was, in fact, a lure; he wanted to maneuver the enemy into attacking him at León, so that he, Villa, could have the benefits Obregón had had at Celaya: trenches, barbed wire, and a short supply line.

As it happened, however, the fight for León turned into a running battle that lasted forty days. The weather turned insufferably hot; the dead of both sides lay unburied, and flies tormented the men of both camps beyond endurance. While *Obregónistas* attacked León, Villa led his cavalry on a roundabout maneuver through the hills to attack other Obregón forces twenty miles to the south, in Silao, and surrounded them. It looked for a brief time like a victory for Villa.

What happened next seemed to promise him almost certain victory. At the beginning of June, on a horseback reconnaissance of his awkward military situation, Obregón

Defeats

was struck by a *Villista* shell. His arm, torn to shreds, was amputated in a field hospital. Later, crazed by the pain, he tried to shoot himself, but the revolver proved empty.

In the meantime his command was given, temporarily, to General Benjamín Hill, another Sonoran like Obregón. It was Hill who had fought Maytorena so bitterly in Sonora, the preceding months. Now, an admirer of his chief, Hill determined to use Obregón's technique of a sudden overpowering blow on an exhausted enemy. He threw all his strength into one surprise assault on Villa's lines; and the men of the *División del Norte*, under terrible fire and surrounded by their own dead, threw away their rifles and ran in panic for the safety of the hills.

By the time Villa reached Aguascalientes, he had counted up the toll of those terrible days. In the fighting at León and Silao and the points between, he had lost in dead, wounded, prisoners, and desertions, eight thousand men.

CHAPTER 24

NOR DID VILLA'S DEFEATS end there. Obregón, driving him steadily north, took Encarnación—a desolate little desert town, but important because of its situation on the railroad. Then he took Aguascalientes, so recently the scene of the Convention which was to have brought peace to the country.

Villa fell back to Zacatecas. But Obregón defeated him there too, and again at San Luis Potosí. Villa was finally forced all the way north to Torreón—and, before summer was out, had to withdraw yet again, losing control of the rich Laguna cotton-growing district. He found himself, at last, in his old stronghold of Chihuahua City.

Meanwhile, early in July, to divert the terrible pounding drive of Obregón's army, he dispatched Rodolfo Fierro on a diversionary action to the south, and this time Fierro more than made up for his recent losses. In a brilliant series of cavalry hits, he retook León, Celaya, and Querétaro, destroying rail lines as he went—and thrust as far south as Pachuca, only seventy miles from the capital.

Alarmed, Carranza's General Pablo González—who by this time was occupying Mexico City—removed his troops. The end of July, González confronted the combined forces of Fierro and Roque González Garza at Jerécuaro, southeast of the still devastated wheatfields of Celaya, and defeated them overwhelmingly. The *Villistas* dragged themselves back to their chief's headquarters with only a fraction of their men, while all their recently won territory along the central railroad fell again to the forces of Obregón and Carranza.

By now, wherever *Villista* forces were engaged, they were suffering defeat. Tomás Urbina, beaten at El Ebano during his attempted march on the Tampico oil fields, lost heart altogether—and loyalty as well. He resigned his commission and headed back to Durango, ostensibly to take up the life of an *hacendado* at Las Nieves.

But near the end of that terrible summer, word reached Villa that Urbina had taken with him some million pesos of his army's payroll—and, still worse, was planning to go over to Carranza.

Villa could, perhaps, have forgiven the theft. He could not forgive the possibility, even the hint, of another betrayal. In mid-September, he set out with Rodolfo Fierro and two hundred men, to revenge himself on his oldest friend.

After leaving the train at Mapimí, the end of the line, he and his escort rode over high rocky desert to the cultivated land of northern Durango. Villa had known this part of the state as an outlaw, when he had first left his lonely life in the sierra to join with two other *bandidos*. Not far off, now, was one of the ranch houses of the *hacienda* Canutillo, which he had ridden past in the night, all those years ago, with a herd of stolen mules. Here was the river, swollen by summer rains, which irrigated the fields—and abruptly, in the midst of a flatland, one could make out the village and *hacienda* of Las Nieves, a cluster of low adobe houses built fortress-like around a central compound.

Villa's last visit here, to celebrate the christening of

Urbina's baby daughter, had been a wild and joyous affair, with cockfights in the compound, and dancing, and *barbacoa*, and a band playing almost continuously. He and Urbina had talked of old times; and Urbina, his little eyes looking wise in that leathery brown face of his, had warned him to be careful of Carranza. That had been hardly more than a year ago. Now Urbina was planning to join up with the old badger!

The charge on the *hacienda* took Urbina's guard by complete surprise. There was a burst of gunfire; bullets ricocheted off the adobe walls of the compound—and within minutes, the place was in Villa's hands, and Urbina lay felled with a bullet in him, begging to talk to his old friend alone for a few minutes.

Villa, grim, helped him into one of the inner rooms. But his anger, which had survived the long trip here, was not proof against Urbina's pleas. In a few minutes he came out and gave orders for Urbina to be taken to the hospital in Chihuahua.

Fierro was furious. He had known this would happen. He insisted that Urbina was a traitor and must be shot. At last, reluctantly, Villa reversed himself again, and allowed Fierro to carry out the execution.

Later, it was said, Fierro almost took the *hacienda* apart, looking for Urbina's "treasure." He found it, the story went, and helped himself to as much gold and silver as he could carry.

That summer of 1915 saw the end of many men who had figured in the Revolution—on both sides. Porfirio Díaz had died in July, in Paris. Young Luisito's brother Eugenio Aguirre Benavides, who had deserted Villa to follow Gutiérrez, had been killed by the *Carrancistas*. "Big ears" Maclovio Herrera had been killed at Nuevo Laredo.

And in Texas, Victoriano Huerta was in jail. During the

Defeats

early months of the First World War, the former dictator had been conspiring with German agents in Spain. He had left Europe for New York, and there, unaware that he was under constant surveillance by American Intelligence officials, had received enough money from his German contact to finance a fresh invasion of Mexico. The invaders—anti-Revolutionary exiles like himself, Felix Díaz, and Pascual Orozco—would, of course, set up a government friendly to Germany. However, before Huerta could cross the border, the Americans had seized him; and now he lay in an El Paso prison hospital, ill of a wasting disease.

The illness was variously diagnosed; but considering that Huerta had not been sober a day in his adult life, it was probably cirrhosis of the liver. He would die in January of 1916.

The many-times-turncoat Pascual Orozco had also been arrested in El Paso. Before long, he would escape, and be killed by Texas Rangers.

But these were Villa's enemies, men for whom he would waste few tears. In mid-October, only three weeks after the killing of Tomás Urbina, Villa lost his brutal—but indispensable—friend Rodolfo Fierro.

It happened near the ruins of Casas Grandes, where heavy rains had filled the rivers to overflowing and turned sandy flatlands into treacherous mud. Villa's men, on their way to Sonora for a campaign, had been held up on the shores of a flooded *laguna*. Fierro, in the vanguard, tried to take a shortcut across what seemed a sandbar—and found himself and his horse sinking into quicksand. Burdened by heavy boots, cartridge belt—and, it was said among the soldiers, by a moneybelt filled with the gold he had taken from the dead Urbina—he sank, flailing about helplessly, out of sight.

It must have come as the crowning blow to Villa, who only four days before had suffered the bitterest political setback he had known since the beginning of the Revolution. On October 19th, 1915, the United States government had formally recognized the government of Venustiano Carranza.

Several months before, in June, President Woodrow Wilson had issued an urgent plea to all the warring factions in Mexico. The country, he said, was "apparently no nearer a solution of her tragic troubles than she was when the Revolution was first kindled."

It was true. There were battles like brushfires, everywhere one looked. "Her crops are destroyed," said Wilson. "Her fields lie unseeded, her work cattle are confiscated for the use of the armed factions, her people flee to the mountains to escape being drawn into unavailing bloodshed . . ." He urged the dissidents to unite, and implied that if they could not, his own government might be forced to intervene.

Villa, Zapata, and with one exception every other leader, were eager to negotiate; but Carranza, as he had so often done before, played a delaying action. What was there to negotiate? His regime was the only legitimate government of Mexico, he said, and he now controlled seven-eighths of the country anyway.

Villa, still putting up a last-ditch action against recognition of the First Chief, decried Carranza's claim. "He has not even the form of a government," he protested, at a press conference in Ciudad Juárez. ". . . To recognize Carranza is to invite anarchy in our country!"

But since the battles of Celaya and León, it was clear that Villa's military might was destroyed. Too, even the most sympathetic Americans could no longer condone his hot-tempered "executions" of prisoners and political enemies.

And the shooting of William Benton still lingered in many minds. Dealing with Pancho Villa was indeed, as young Guzmán had said, like handling dynamite.

Meanwhile, disorders continued unabated. In Mexico City during one three-week period in July and August, the government changed hands five times. The soldiers of *Carrancista* Pablo González, chasing Zapata through the hills and valleys of Morelos, were committing depredations against *haciendas*, refineries, and citizens more ruthless and destructive than the *Zapatistas* had ever wrought. And bands of Mexicans—including some *Carrancista* soldiers—were making frequent raids across the Rio Grande into Texas.

Moreover, Washington had been thoroughly alarmed at Huerta's dealings with the German agents. The Americans knew, with the European war spreading daily, that it was imperative to have a stable government on their own southern border. And in spite of Carranza's utter disregard for democratic procedure, his government did seem to offer the highest degree of stability.

The Americans' recognition of Carranza was disastrous enough, in Villa's eyes. But even more damaging was the arms embargo that accompanied it. Henceforth, declared Woodrow Wilson, no Mexican leader save Carranza could buy arms or ammunition from the United States. Now Villa would be truly crippled.

But he refused to accept defeat. His move toward Sonora, which had cost Fierro his life, was an attempt to reach and combine with the forces of Maytorena; to capture and hold at least that portion of the frontier, and from there, to start a southland sweep once more. It was Villa's last great, desperate drive.

Initially, perhaps, he had some reason for hope. He still had a certain amount of ammunition and six thousand men;

late in October, he and his soldiers began their western march.

Unfortunately, winter had come early; and as they started up the sierras, the torrential rains turned to snows and then to blizzards. His men were not prepared for such weather; many died of exposure. Ragged, exhausted, half-starving, the others pushed through blizzard-swept Púlpito Pass, and then straggled down the slopes on the farther side. At Agua Prieta, on the Mexico-Arizona border, they met the army of Plutarco Elías Calles, the *Carrancista* general who, with Benjamín Hill, had been holding Sonora all these months against the forces of Maytorena.

It was a brief, and bloody, battle. Calles was an inferior tactician, but he had an abundance of men and supplies. After a day's terrible pounding, the *Villistas* sought shelter in the darkness—only to be picked out by giant searchlights from the American side of the border, which blinded them, revealed their positions, and made their further destruction by Calles's guns an easy matter.

Bitter, furious at the Americans, Villa moved what was left of his men south toward Hermosillo, the capital of Sonora. There was a brief battle en route, at Alamito; and on November 22nd, he attacked Hermosillo. His army was all but wiped out.

There was nothing to do now but go back the way they had come. The return trip across the sierra, in the very depth of winter now, was even more devastating than it had been before. By the time Villa reached Chihuahua he had fewer than six hundred men, of the six thousand he had begun the campaign with.

Before the year's end, Ciudad Juárez too had fallen to the *Carrancistas*—and all but one of Villa's few remaining garrisons as well. He had no more territory to govern; his *bilimbiques* were all but worthless; he had almost no ammunition. By New Year's Day, 1916, he withdrew from his last stronghold at Chihuahua City, to disappear with a tiny group of followers into the hills that had sheltered him so many times before.

CHAPTER 25

VILLA'S REVOLUTION HAD been preempted—by Carranza's words, if not by his deeds. Death and desertion had thinned his army to a mere shadow. Of all his old leaders, only Felipe Angeles was still loyal, and Angeles was in the United States now, hopelessly pleading Villa's cause.

But there was one trade Villa still knew well—cattle rustling. And there was one emotion that could still fire his blood: revenge.

In those first dark months of 1916, he returned to his old life of banditry to support himself and his remaining followers. He led a few scattered raids on small towns or *haciendas*, seizing horses, ammunition, and supplies; then, on January 10th, near Santa Isabel in Chihuahua, some of his men stopped a train carrying a group of mining engineers to a mine at Cusi.

The other passengers were robbed. The Americans, however, were taken from the train and shot.

The next month found Villa's men raiding one of the huge *ranchos* of American newspaper publisher William Randolph Hearst. It was a most provocative action.

Why? Because Villa wanted to prove to the United States

that Carranza could not, after all, promise a peaceful and unified Mexico? Or because he, Villa, could not forgive the American arms embargo and those searchlights flooding the field at Agua Prieta, two months ago in Sonora? Whatever the reason—and in spite of the demand in every Hearst newspaper that the Americans "plant the American flag all the way to the Panama Canal"—early March found Villa on the move once more.

This time, he was traveling with about five hundred men toward Palomas, on the near side of the border, facing Columbus, New Mexico.

To be sure, a United States cavalry unit was stationed at Columbus, with its wealth of horses, arms, and ammunition. Too, there was a merchant living there who had once defaulted on a delivery of ammunition to Villa. Otherwise, it was an anonymous little town, in the midst of a dry plain, its main road merely a wagon-rut crossing the railroad tracks. It had two hotels, one bank, a theater, a few stores, and a handful of frame or adobe houses. It hardly seemed a target worth attacking.

Nevertheless, at 4:30 one pitch-black morning, an American army private on sentinel duty surprised a group of Mexican horsemen riding silently into town. He tried to give the alarm, and they shot him.

The silence shattered, cries of "*Viva* Villa!" filled the air, and suddenly, *Villistas* were everywhere, shouting, shooting, setting fires, breaking down doors to gain entrance. The defaulting hardware dealer was sought, found absent, and his store destroyed. Terrified residents fled to the mesquite; some even hid in outhouses. The cavalry's machine guns were brought hurriedly into action, barking out an answer to the Mexicans' rifle fire. Twenty-four Americans were killed, and scores of *Villistas*.

By morning the invaders were in flight; the American cavalry pursued them over the border and fifteen miles into Chihuahua before losing them.

Villa had not accompanied his men into the town; as in the train raid, he had remained at a little distance behind. But the plan was his.

Woodrow Wilson announced that he would send troops through Chihuahua to track down Villa. Carranza insisted that Mexico be allowed to take care of the outlaws its own way, without intervention. But a week after the raid, two cavalry units, one commanded by United States Brigadier General John J. Pershing, were crossing the border into Chihuahua with orders to get Villa, dead or alive.

It became open season on Mexicans in every border town in Texas, and notes between the United States and the Carranza government heated up almost to the point of war. General Pershing and his "Punitive Expedition," however, searched the Chihuahua plains and deserts in a hopeless hunt for Villa. Fifteen thousand cavalrymen, supported by army engineers, signal corpsmen, infantry, field artillerymen, and eight biplanes, could not find him.

Nor would the *Carrancistas* help them. They hated the foreign invaders far more than they hated Villa.

Actually, Villa was engaged, soon after, in a raid on *Carrancista* troops near Ciudad Guerrero. He had been wounded below the right knee, and spirited off by wagon into the hills. When the wagon broke down, he was carried by litter to a cave deep in the sierra, where his men tried to treat the wound with strips of nopal cactus. They removed the bullet without anaesthetic; and as his leather-tough body fought the fever and he drifted in and out of delirium, they fought the gangrene.

Word reached the Americans of his whereabouts. American soldiers combed that portion of the hills—coming so close, on one occasion, that Villa could hear their voices. But the face of the cave was shielded by brush, and they did not find him.

Within two months, the gangrene was checked and the bone mended, and he could walk again. By prearrangement he met with his followers in July at San Juan Batista; and by mid-September, his ranks swelled by countrymen infuriated at the American cavalry's presence, he attacked and captured Chihuahua City.

It seemed, for a few hours, like one of Villa's Revolutionary conquests of old. He issued a statement blaming Carranza for allowing intervention, and demanded an election, social reforms, and the expulsion of all foreign land- and mine-owners.

But his seizure of the city was, after all, a token act; he left it before nightfall, with sixteen carloads of arms and ammunition he had captured. In November he seized it again, and this time held it for a week. Then he won, and lost, Torreón. But these were the final flare-ups of a dream that was doomed. By early January, 1917, he was again reduced to sporadic raids on *haciendas* in Durango and Chihuahua. He was once more a bandit, without the dignity of a cause.

In February of 1917, General Pershing's troops went home. The United States was being drawn closer to the war in Europe; she needed her soldiers for more important business than playing hide-and-seek with a Mexican outlaw through the Chihuahua hills.

Meanwhile, Venustiano Carranza had taken one constructive step toward stabilizing the political situation. In the autumn of 1916 he had ordered special elections for a constitutional convention to be held in Querétaro.

Carranza saw himself as a sort of latter-day Benito Juárez; and the idea of a "Carranza Constitution" appealed to his vanity. He wanted such a document, however, to strengthen the authority of the President, not to promulgate reforms. Indeed, his General González was still chasing the peasant-soldiers of Zapata through the hills of Morelos because they insisted on land reform. And, with Mexico City in the grip of a series of strikes, he was growing more and more antitrade union, and had decreed the death penalty for strike leaders.

But the delegates who convened in Querétaro were not of the same mind as their chief. Under the leadership of Alvaro Obregón, who was by now Carranza's Minister of War, a determined group of liberals and radicals managed to insert a few articles in the new draft of laws which turned it from a purely political to an impressive social document.

The new Constitution's Article 27 declared that the Mexican nation was the original owner of all land, water, and minerals, and had the right to grant concessions for their use—which could be revoked at any time. The nation likewise had the right to expropriate and distribute all such holdings. All the communal lands, the *ejidos,* which had been taken from the villagers, were to be returned. All Church properties were to be nationalized, and federal and state governments would draw up plans for redistribution of land.

Article 123 was a bill of rights for the workers. Although in the immediate years to follow it would be all but ignored, it was one of the most enlightened pieces of legislation for its time anywhere in the world. It provided for an eight-hour day; the abolition of child labor; workmen's compensation for accidents or dismissal without cause; maternity care for working mothers and schools for their children; the end of peonage; and the right to bargain collectively and to strike.

Although the Constitution of 1857 had attempted to restrict the power of the Church, several articles in the new document went further. Marriage was to be a civil contract; divorce was legalized; alien priests were forbidden the pulpit and Mexican priests were denied control of primary schools

Defeats

and the right to form political parties. Curiously, most of the delegates who approved these articles were good Catholics; but they recognized the need for complete separation of Church and state.

Still another article outlawed capital punishment for political offenses—giving hope that the years of political killings would end.

Although the new Constitution went much further than Carranza wanted it to, he signed it. He simply neglected to enforce it. But the laws would remain on the books, a beacon lighting the way for future generations of Mexicans.

The Constitution drafted, and peace of a sort established, Obregón began to ponder his plans for the future. He neither liked nor trusted the men surrounding Carranza. He might have run against his chief in the special elections to be held that March of 1917. But he had been persuaded not to, in the interests of peace and unity, by his old friend Adolfo de la Huerta, now provisional governor of Sonora. After all, as De la Huerta had pointed out, Obregón was still a relatively young man—and there would be another election in a few years.

So, the day that Venustiano Carranza was inaugurated as President, Obregón resigned his post in the Cabinet and went home to his farm in Sonora. He had given one arm and six years of his life to the cause of Mexican progress. Perhaps, for the time being, that was enough. And perhaps Mexico's very longing for peace and social justice would bring it about —Venustiano Carranza notwithstanding.

CHAPTER 26

BUT THERE WAS NOT social justice. Not yet.

To be sure, Carranza expropriated certain large holdings—thirty million acres, of which he gave less than a sixteenth to the Indians and *campesinos*. Even then, more often than not, the recipients had neither water nor seed; many lacked even tools to till the ground. Much of the rest of the acreage went to Carranza's generals and political supporters. And, because the *Zapatistas* continued to protest this state of affairs, General Pablo González went on hunting them down, all through Morelos.

The labor unions had hoped to gain strength from the new Constitution. Instead, they now found themselves persecuted by local and state officials, and many union leaders were jailed.

And there were fewer schools in operation under Carranza than there had been under Díaz. Carranza did away with the Ministry of Education, leaving the problem of school financing to the states and local communities—which had so little money that many of the schools were forced to shut down.

And, though Carranza himself continued to lead an upright, almost Spartan life, his supporters plundered the people and government alike. Civil service jobs were sold to the highest bidder; and widows of the Revolution were forced to pay kickbacks to petty bureaucrats before they could draw their pensions. As for Pablo González—when he was not off in Morelos chasing Zapata, he spent so much time building his own ill-gotten fortune in Mexico City that he became known as the "bandit with a necktie." Also, it was suspected that he had a hand in the organization known as the "gray automobile gang"—a group of men who drove about the city robbing and shooting at will.

It was small wonder that when the Sonoran general, Plutarco Elías Calles, joined the Cabinet late in 1919, he resigned in disgust almost immediately. Carranza's government, he said, was "the most corrupt administration in the history of Mexico."

Nor was there peace in the countryside. Villa continued to make sudden raids on *haciendas* and towns in the north, through these years of 1917, '18, and early '19, replenishing his supplies of food and ammunition, and steadily increasing the size of his striking force. There was dissatisfaction elsewhere, too, and violence. There were uprisings of the Maya Indians in Yucatán. The state of Oaxaca declared its independence, and the territory of Baja California tried to. And, as they had been doing for years, oil companies in the states of Tamaulipas and Veracruz, on the Atlantic coast, were still making enormous payoffs to a bandit general named Manuel Peláez. He, in return, refrained from raiding them, and kept government tax collectors at bay.

Meanwhile, for the people of Morelos, life continued to be tragic. Although the *Zapatistas* had burned down *haciendas* in an attempt to regain land they felt belonged to them, they had behaved, for the most part, like farmers. At planting and harvesting time, they had always gone back to their patches of soil, returning to Zapata's army at his call. And they had tried to preserve the rice and cane fields and the sugar refineries, feeling that these rightfully belonged to the people. But González's men showed no such compunction. They burned and pillaged fields and orchards, destroying crops to starve the Morelians into submission. They leveled the sugar refineries, and with almost primitive savagery, destroyed every *hacienda* the *Zapatistas* had left standing. Control of the state's capital, Cuernavaca, and the towns of Cuautla, Ayala, and Jojutla, seesawed back and forth between the contending forces.

Throughout the hostilities, the *Zapatistas* continued to make public accusations against Carranza for the corruption of his regime, for his failure to live up to his Revolutionary promises, and for his authoritarianism. As long as he was at the helm, it was clear they would not cease their fight; they would continue to heed Zapata's cry: "Men of the South, it is better to die on your feet than live on your knees!"

Carranza's and González's nightmare, during this period, was that Zapata and Obregón might join forces against the government. Also, the opening months of 1919, people in Mexico City were beginning to speculate about a possible successor to Carranza; and Pablo González had begun to think of himself as a candidate. Hence, when Carranza ordered him to find and kill Zapata at all costs, González was eager to oblige.

It was decided that where an army had failed, treachery might succeed. Accordingly, González laid plans to lead Zapata into an ambush. He began by rigging evidence that one of his colonels, Jesús María Guajardo, was dissatisfied with the present regime and wanted to join Zapata's forces.

The cautious peasant leader waited for evidence that Guajardo, who could offer him a goodly supply of arms and ammunition, was acting in good faith. As proof, Guajardo raided a small *Carrancista* garrison in the valley of Morelos; there were casualties on both sides. Zapata was convinced.

An appointment for a meeting between Zapata and the

Defeats

new "convert" was set up for April 10th, at the *hacienda* Chinameca, Guajardo's headquarters. Zapata, having left his own hideout in the predawn darkness and ridden several hours to the meeting place, was welcomed by a flourish of trumpets. He left his guard outside, in case of a surprise attack, and rode into the compound of the *hacienda* to meet Guajardo—and was mown down.

His bullet-ridden body was taken on the back of a horse to the town of Cuautla, where it was dumped on the floor of the Municipal Palace. It lay on display for days, to prove to the Morelians that their beloved leader was really dead, and that it was useless now to go on fighting.

For the Indians of Morelos, it was a tragic loss. Emiliano Zapata had been the one truly revolutionary general the years of war had produced—the one leader who had fought not for wealth, or power, or revenge, but only for land for his people.

Carranza received Pablo González's report of the ambush "with satisfaction." He made Guajardo a general, and gave him a reward of fifty thousand pesos.

But however grateful he was to Pablo González for conceiving the plot, he did not choose him as his successor for the next year's elections.

Meanwhile, encouraged by the success of his guerrilla strikes in Durango and Chihuahua, Villa had sent word to Felipe Angeles to come back from the United States and join him in a "Liberal Alliance." With Angeles as tactician, perhaps the hard-riding *Villista* cavalry could take the initiative in a southward sweep, taking everything before them, as they had done before.

The gentle Angeles, so unlike his chief and yet so loyal, had responded. He reentered Mexico in December, 1918; and by April of 1919, he and Villa had captured Parral. In mid-June they took Ciudad Juárez; but Villa's presence on the border so alarmed the "Colossus of the North" that American troops intervened again, crossing the border in strength to drive the *Villistas* out.

In mid-November, Villa suffered the last great loss of his life. Felipe Angeles was caught in the mountains of Chihuahua, near the "Valley of the Olive Trees," by a *Carrancista* patrol. He was taken to Chihuahua City, where he was tried and sentenced to be shot.

His military genius and his gentle dignity had won him admirers all over Mexico, and Carranza was deluged by pleas to spare his life. The pleas were ignored. Angeles went to his grave, however, without fear, without bitterness. The night before he was to face the firing squad, he had written:

"I know my death will further the cause of democracy, because great causes are enriched by the blood of martyrs."

Earlier that year, Carranza had chosen a candidate for the 1920 elections—his amiable, anonymous ambassador to Washington, Ignacio Bonillas. The Americans liked him, but few Mexicans had ever heard of him.

There were protests. Because of his popularity in the United States, Mexicans referred to him as "*Meester* Bonillas." But Carranza, knowing he dared not violate the "no reelection" principle, also knew that with a puppet in the presidency he could continue to rule from behind the scenes. He stood by his choice.

Alvaro Obregón, hearing of the selection, reacted with amusement. Bonillas, he said, was a nice enough fellow. In fact, he said, "the world has lost a first-rate bookkeeper." And he promptly declared his own candidacy.

But when he embarked upon a vote-getting campaign across the country, he found out it would not be easy to defy Carranza's wishes. Madero's old plea of "effective suffrage" was, it seemed, a laughingstock; already, in half-a-dozen state elections, there had been open fraud.

His train was frequently detained for no apparent reason, so he missed speaking engagements. And in some parts of the countryside, his campign workers were hanged or shot.

Reaching Mexico City, Obregón found he was under police surveillance every moment. His dwelling was watched, his car followed.

He recognized the telltale signs. For decades, it had been a saying in Mexico that "Presidential ambition is a disease which usually ends fatally," and he knew he must escape the city.

By a ruse, he managed to get away from an automobile pursuing him, hid in the park, and at last made his way to the house of a friend. Later, dressed as a brakeman, with a coat over his shoulder to hide the empty arm-flap of his jacket, he and his friend Benjamín Hill took a train bound for the tropical state of Guerrero, to the south.

Carranza, furious at his opponent's escape, telegraphed the train's escort that Obregón was to be arrested and executed.

However, Obregón jumped the train, and managed to reach his destination by other means. From Guerrero, in the sleepy little state capital of Chilpancingo, he announced late in April, 1920, that there was no alternative but to take up arms against the Carranza government.

Simultaneously, leaders in Sonora took the same stand. Sonora's governor Adolfo de la Huerta proclaimed the state's independence; Plutarco Elías Calles was declared head of a new army, and the old military sweep down the coastal states of the Pacific began again.

From then on, things moved swiftly. By the end of April, thirteen Mexican states were in rebellion against the government; and even Pablo González, knowing a lost cause when he saw one, declared against his old chief.

By May 6th, Venustiano Carranza was in dignified flight from Mexico City, along with ten thousand followers and all the gold and silver in the national treasury—more than four million pesos' worth. Aboard one of hundreds of trains which were leaving the capital, he set out for Veracruz.

He would not reach it.

En route, in the mountainous regions of Tlaxcala and Puebla, fighting broke out along the tracks, and the trains could not get through. Obregón sent a telegram offering a safe conduct, but Carranza ignored it. He, and a small escort of soldiers and cadets, then set out on horseback and afoot, deeper into the wilds of northern Puebla.

Here he was met by a "friendly" native and led to the "safety" of a remote Indian village, where he was given a hut to sleep in. In the darkness an hour or two before dawn, his hut was invaded, and he was filled with bullets.

The officers responsible, arrested and brought for trial to Mexico City, insisted he had committed suicide.

Three days after Carranza's death, Adolfo de la Huerta, who had frequently tried to conciliate among the Revolution's warring factions, was appointed interim President by the Mexican Congress. That summer of 1920, he received a letter from an old friend—Pancho Villa.

In the interests of his country's peace, said Villa, he wanted to extend a warm *abrazo* to De la Huerta and generals Obregón, Calles, and Hill. "If you are ashamed to be my friends," he said, "reject me . . . [But] if you would deal honorably with me, send me a letter signed by all of you . . . Meanwhile, I am suspending hostilities."

Obregón had honest misgivings about Villa and did not respond. Calles, however, who had a deep-grained hatred of Villa, telegraphed one of his generals to seek out and attack the outlaw chieftain.

Villa intercepted the telegram. He escaped the plot, but it made him wary. Late in July, he and his men made one final raid—on the cypress-shaded little railroad town of Sabinas, in northern Coahuila—and then, from a position of greater strength, wired De la Huerta that he was ready to negotiate, but with him, and him alone.

Since the battles of Sonora, particularly the one at Agua Prieta, with those American searchlights picking out his position, he had disliked Calles; the recent plot against him only fortified that dislike. But "Adolfito" de la Huerta had always been his friend; perhaps, with "'Fito" at the helm now, he felt the Revolution was in good hands at last.

Or perhaps Villa, like Mexico itself, was worn out with war and bloodshed. In any event, the fight for Sabinas was his last. No other town, no other *hacienda*, would know that moment of terror in the night, the sounds of hoofbeats and gunfire and the wild voices yelling "*Viva* Villa!" out of the darkness. The "Centaur of the North" would never make another raid.

PART SEVEN

The Tamed Puma

CHAPTER 27

IT WAS SUMMER, 1920. Ten years of civil war had left Mexico a shattered country. Successive armies had swept across the cultivated fields, destroying or commandeering the harvests. Millions of head of cattle had been slaughtered to feed the soldiers of both sides, or had been sold abroad to provide money for armaments. Irrigation ditches had been turned into trenches, terraced hillsides into gun emplacements; houses were battered ruins. People in city and country had suffered hunger and disease. Weakened as they were, they were easy prey to the worldwide epidemic of influenza, which killed a million and a quarter Mexicans. And there was hardly a family which had not lost a father, a son, or a brother in one or another of the great battles.

There had to be peace. The nation could not survive more warfare.

It was in this climate of desperation that Pancho Villa and Adolfo de la Huerta arrived at their agreement. Villa and his men would put down their arms, though Villa would be allowed a personal escort of fifty soldiers. In exchange, he would receive from the government twenty-five thousand acres of the Canutillo lands in northern Durango, some of which had previously belonged to Tomás Urbina. His men would receive lands at Río Conchos as well as a year's military pay; and Villa would be given a large cash sum in lieu of his salary as a general—a half-million pesos, rumor said. It seemed, in the long run, a fair price to pay for peace.

From Sabinas, Villa started his last long ride, at the head of his fifty-man escort. They rode across deserts, plains, and hills they had fought for time and again the last ten years. They rode through towns Villa had taken two or three times; past stretches of railroad he had destroyed, or rebuilt, or traveled along with his boxcars of troops, artillery, and horses. Through Coahuila they rode, to Chihuahua; over the border into Durango—and finally, to the *hacienda* Canutillo.

There, the former peon now turned *hacendado*, Villa set about creating a model agricultural settlement. He poured his boundless energy into making his land productive. He invested large sums in modern equipment, and cleared the ground with heavy tractors. He plowed and planted, restored the stock, and rebuilt the big old house. He even imported an American farm manager who taught him and his men contour plowing and crop rotation.

He established a bank for low-interest loans to small farmers. He built a school for the *hacienda* children; and he spent hours at night laboriously teaching himself arithmetic, history, and economics. He could not forget that he had been twenty-five years old before he could write his own name.

As for his domestic life—by now, he had at least three "wives," to whom he was "legally" married. Each was carefully established in a different city, and to each of them he was faithful—in his fashion. Half-a-dozen of his children lived with him at the *hacienda*. He was mellow, and happy; the hot-tempered Villa of old had vanished.

The Tamed Puma

For three years, his farmland prospered, and the herds of cattle he had bought grazed the fields and grew fat.

Farther south, his friend De la Huerta, during his brief six months in office, had also succeeded in neutralizing the *Zapatistas*. In exchange for laying down their arms, they were promised ownership of the land they had taken. Thus, Morelos became the first state of Mexico to win land redistribution.

Elections were held, and on November 30th, 1920, Alvaro Obregón was inaugurated as President. He had been a firm believer in the aims of the Revolution, but he also had an instinct for politics as the "art of the possible." As chief executive, his moves were cautious and practical. On land reform, he proceeded slowly; about three million acres were given to the people of six hundred twenty-four villages. And there was still too little attention paid to the villagers' needs for water and low-interest credit for seed and tools.

To make sure he did not antagonize the former owners of the expropriated lands, Obregón repaid them with government bonds. What holder of such bonds would revolt against the government that issued them?

And while he respected the rights of labor to organize, he encouraged foreign investment and the creation of new industries.

There were still, of course, the generals. Mexico City swarmed with them. But Obregón tolerated their parasitic existence because he did not want a barracks revolt on his hands.

Only in the field of education did he make a giant stride forward. He reestablished the Ministry of Education, with philosopher José Vasconcelos at its head; more than a thousand rural schools were built during his term of office.

Vasconcelos also found a way to bring Mexico's history to the illiterate. Murals showing the Spanish conquest, Independence, the wars of the Reform, and the Revolution, blossomed on the walls of public buildings; and such painters as Diego Rivera, José Clemente Orozco, and David Alfaro Siqueiros became world famous. Those years, and the decade following, saw a flowering of Mexican art.

The new Constitution, whatever its other virtues, made no provision for a two-party system; and the incumbent President's choice for successor could be virtually sure of election. By 1923, it became apparent that the strongest man in Obregón's Cabinet, and therefore his undoubted successor, was not the sober, dedicated Adolfo de la Huerta, but Obregón's fellow soldier from Sonora, Plutarco Elías Calles. Calles was known to be more radical in terms of labor unions and land distribution; but he was also dictatorial and intolerant of opposition. As he emerged as the candidate-to-be, there were stirrings of dissatisfaction in the capital and elsewhere; and even that man of peace, De la Huerta, was concerned about the direction the country might take under Calles.

It was generally assumed that if a serious, open quarrel were to break out between the two presidential hopefuls, Pancho Villa would side with De la Huerta. Politicians wondered if he might take up arms again, in support of his friend. He had vowed not to. But where Villa was concerned, no one could be absolutely sure about anything.

Nor would they ever be quite sure who was responsible for what happened in Parral, Chihuahua, that morning of July 20th, 1923.

Villa had driven up there from Canutillo the day before, in his new Dodge touring car, to transact some business and to attend the christening of the baby of one of his old followers. It had been an ordinary, pleasant summer's day.

He had spent the night at a hotel he owned; and, quite early next morning, accompanied by six companions—his

The Tamed Puma

plump secretary Miguel Trillo, his regular chauffeur, and four members of his escort—he had set off at the wheel of the Dodge. Near one of the town plazas, a street vendor had called out to him, "*Viva* Villa!" and then made a hand signal, in the direction of a nearby house. From behind a wall of the house seven men emerged, their guns blazing. The car swerved wildly and slammed into a tree. The seven men came running toward it, still firing.

In the moments before he died, Villa managed to draw his pistol and kill one of his attackers. One of Villa's comrades, hideously wounded, managed to make his escape; the other five were killed.

The assassins withdrew without haste. They seemed to know they would not be arrested. They were right.

It was noised about, soon after, that the leader of the assassins was a man named Lozoya, who had long had a grudge against Villa. But he was not the intellectual author of the killings. Who was, then?

Within two weeks, a local politician named Jesús Salas Barraza proclaimed that the plan had been his, in punishment for Villa's many crimes. Early in August he presented himself for judgment in Mexico City, where he was imprisoned for a short while, then released.

But still, no one was sure that he had acted without inspiration from someone else. The governor of Chihuahua was an old military foe of Villa. So was the future President, Plutarco Elías Calles . . .

Salas Barraza denied that Calles had had anything to do with the killing. He went on denying it until he died, thirty years later.

On the other hand, in 1924, a certain Colonel Lara of the military garrison at Parral told a newspaperman about having been called down to Mexico City for an interview with Calles, some months prior to the assassination. Calles, he said, had asked him to get rid of the former outlaw; and Lara had returned to Chihuahua, to seek out people who had old grudges against Villa . . .

Who knows? Perhaps it *had* been Calles's plan. How else could the assassins have obtained the government-issued bullets which had killed Villa and his friends?

No one would ever be sure.

Villa's death was not the last political assassination in post-Revolutionary Mexico. But it was almost the last. The temper of the country, slowly but surely, was changing.

One of the final eruptions of violence occurred late in 1923. Adolfo de la Huerta was persuaded to resign from Obregón's Cabinet; and, in December, a number of men with motives both selfish and unselfish joined him in revolt against the "imposition" of Calles as presidential candidate.

The uprising was crushed after three months of bloody fighting; De la Huerta fled to the United States; and the following summer, Calles was voted into office.

He and his successor faced scattered uprisings, subsequently, of groups of militant Catholics, known as *Cristeros*. Obregón had avoided pressing the anti-clerical laws of the new Constitution, but Calles enforced them, and over the next several years there were armed outbreaks throughout the country in protest, with bands of *Cristeros* attacking Protestants, labor leaders, and rural schoolteachers.

In 1928 there was one more political assassination.

Alvaro Obregón had just been elected again to the presidency; but three weeks later, a fanatically religious young artist—whom the Catholics, shocked and horrified, were quick to disclaim—followed him one Sunday afternoon to a San Angel restaurant and there, on the pretense of sketching his portrait, shot him.

The madness of the act was, it seemed, the catharsis the nation needed. President Calles immediately announced that

The Tamed Puma

Mexico would never again allow itself to rely so heavily on the leadership of any single man.

Not until the presidency of Michoacán's former governor Lázaro Cárdenas in 1934, however, would the ideals of the new Constitution truly be implemented. It was Cárdenas who would distribute to the peasants twice as much land as all his predecessors together. It was he who, when foreign oil companies refused to bargain with their Mexican workers, invoked Article 123 of the Constitution, bringing Mexico's subsoil wealth back into Mexican hands. And it was during his regime that countless Mexican intellectuals, who had fled into exile over disagreements with preceding presidents, were able to come home at last.

The problem of poverty was not solved, nor is it yet; much remained to be done. But hundreds of thousands of *campesinos* now worked their own land, who once would have been peons on the great *haciendas*. And the atmosphere of open oppression and violence, which had made revolution inevitable, was ended.

What, in the long run, had Pancho Villa contributed to this achievement? And were the gains, for the poor of Mexico, enough to justify the thousands of deaths that resulted from the strife between Villa and the other Revolutionary leaders?

Who can judge? There is no scales that can weigh the good and bad of that giant of a man. His unbridled acts of love and hate, of generosity and vengefulness, were all out-sized— a part, perhaps, of the time and place in which he lived. His tragedy was that having helped make a revolution, he could not help solve it. He had shared in the destruction of an old way of life; he did not know how to build a new one.

But no one whose life he had ever touched, however briefly, would ever forget him: the excitement in those extraordinary amber-colored eyes; the bowed legs and the powerful body; the wide, sudden grin, crinkling the windburned face.

"But when you met him," young men would ask the old ones, in years to come, "what was it like? How did you *feel?*"

"How did I feel?" Old men would pause, remembering. "I liked him. That was how I felt. I *liked* him!"

GLOSSARY

abrazo: an embrace, a brotherly hug
arriero: muleteer
arroyo: gully; dry watercourse

bandido: bandit
    bandido número uno: number one bandit
barbacoa: barbecued meat
barranca: ravine
bilimbiques: (sl.) unsupported paper money

cacique: political boss or tyrant of Indian village
calabozo: prison
campesino: peasant or small farmer
cantina: saloon
Carrancista: soldier or follower of Venustiano Carranza
Casas Grandes: Big Houses (pre-Hispanic ruins in Chihuahua)
centavo: smallest Mexican coin, worth 1/100 of a peso
charro: cowboy
    charro costume: embroidered cowboy suit for special occasions

científico: advocate of government as a science
ciudad: city
ciudadela: citadel, armory
Colorado: member of Pascual Orozco's forces, a "red-flagger"
comandante: commander, major
comida: food, midday meal
compadre: close friend
compañero: companion, friend
   compañerito: little friend
coup: (Fr.) blow, quick military uprising against government
creole: native-born, of whatever parentage
Cristero: militant Catholic of the 1920s
Cucaracha, La: Villista song "The Cockroach"

democracia: democracy
diez-y-seis: sixteenth; short for the sixteenth of September, Mexico's Independence Day
División del Norte: Division of the North (Villa's)
docena tragica: tragic dozen (usually, the twelve tragic days of Madero's imprisonment)
Dorado: Gilded One; referring to gold braid on uniform of Villa's elite cavalry

ejido: communal village land
   ejidal: adj. describing communal land

Federale: federal soldier
fiesta: party, celebration
filibustero: buccaneer

gringolandia: (sl.) "land of the gringos," referring to the oil lands and installations in Tampico owned by United States interests

Glossary

grito: cry, or shout (Grito: Father Hidalgo's call for independence from Spain)

hacienda: large farm or estate including country house, often with blacksmith, store, granary, etc.
  hacendado: owner of an hacienda
huarache: leather sandal
Huertista: follower of Victoriano Huerta

ley: law
  ley fuga: "law of the fugitive" (i.e. "shot while attempting to escape")
libertad: liberty

Maderista: follower of Francisco Madero
Mañanitas, Las: song played or sung in early morning for birthday, saint's day, or other celebration
mestizo: of mixed Indian and other parentage
Morelianos: people of Morelos

Noche Buena: Christmas Eve
norteño: northerner

Obregónista: follower or soldier of Alvaro Obregón
Orozquistas: followers of Pascual Orozco

padre: father, priest
Palacio Nacional: National Palace, in Mexico City
peon: farmhand or unskilled laborer
peso: Mexican unit of exchange; in Villa's early youth, worth about half a dollar
politico: politician
Porfirista: follower of Porfirio Díaz
pulque: alcoholic drink from the maguey cactus

Quien vive: "Who goes there?" (lit. "Who lives?")

rancho: ranch
    ranchero: rancher or farmer
    ranchito: small farm
río: river
rurale: rural police

señor, señora, señorita: Mr., Mrs., Miss
serape, sarape: blanket used for clothing or bedding
sierra: mountain range
soldadera: soldier's woman

tierra: earth, native land
tortilla: round, flat pancake of ground corn-meal

vaquero: cowhand
Veracruzano: citizen of Veracruz
Villista: follower or soldier of Pancho Villa
Zapatista: follower or soldier of Emiliano Zapata

zócalo: public square

BIBLIOGRAPHY

BRENNER, ANITA. *The Wind that Swept Mexico.* University of Texas Press. Austin, Texas, and London, 1971.

CERVANTES, M. FEDERICO. *Francisco Villa y la Revolución.* Ediciónes Alonso. Mexico, D.F., 1960.

GRUENING, ERNEST. *Mexico and Its Heritage.* Appleton-Century-Crofts, Inc. New York, 1928.

GUZMÁN, MARTÍN LUIS. *The Eagle and the Serpent.* Translated by Harriet de Onis. Dolphin Books, Doubleday & Co., Inc. Garden City, N.Y., 1965.

———. *Memorias de Pancho Villa.* 12th ed. Cia. General de Ediciónes, S.A. Mexico, D.F., 1970.

———. *Memoirs of Pancho Villa.* Translated by Virginia H. Taylor. University of Texas Press. Austin, Texas, and London, 1970.

JOHNSON, WILLIAM WEBER. *Heroic Mexico: The Violent Emergence of a Modern Nation.* Doubleday & Co., Inc. Garden City, N.Y., 1968.

LANDSFORD, WILLIAM DOUGLAS. *Pancho Villa.* Sherbourne Press, Inc. Los Angeles, 1965.

LISTER, FLORENCE C. and ROBERT H. *Chihuahua, Storehouse of Storms.* University of New Mexico Press. Albuquerque, 1966.

LOPEZ, ENRIQUE HANK. "Papa and Pancho Villa," *American Heritage*, Vol. XXI, No. 5. New York, August 1970.

PARKES, HENRY BAMFORD. *A History of Mexico*. Houghton Mifflin Co., The Riverside Press. Boston, 1950.

PUENTE, RAMON. *Villa en Pie*. Editorial Mexico Nuevo. Mexico, D.F., 1937.

O'SHAUGHNESSY, EDITH. *Diplomatic Days*. Harper & Bros. New York and London, 1917.

———. *A Diplomat's Wife in Mexico*. Arno Press and the New York Times. New York, 1970.

TURNER, JOHN KENNETH. *Barbarous Mexico*. University of Texas Press. Austin, Texas, and London, 1969.

Also:

AMERICAN AUTOMOBILE ASSOCIATION. *Mexico and Central America*, 1969–70.

TERRY, PHILIP T. *Terry's Guide to Mexico*. Boston and Hingham.

———. *Same*, edited by James Norman. Doubleday & Co., Inc. Garden City, N.Y., 1965.

I am also indebted to Ramona Uribe Ballesteros, and to Professor Elías Campos Aguilar, for reminiscences of their childhood and youth in Mexico during the Revolution.

3 1701 0005